It
Never
Ends

It
Never
Ends

Mothering Middle-Aged
Daughters

by

SANDRA BUTLER AND NAN FINK GEFEN

SHE WRITES PRESS

Published 2017
Printed in the United States of America
Print ISBN: 978-1-63152-278-9
E-ISBN: 978-1-63152-279-6
Library of Congress Control Number: 2017942937

For information, address:
She Writes Press
1563 Solano Ave #546
Berkeley, CA 94707

Cover design © Julie Metz, Ltd./metzdesign.com
Book design by Stacey Aaronson/thebookdoctorisin.com

She Writes Press is a division of SparkPoint Studio, LLC.

Names and identifying characteristics have been changed to protect the privacy of certain individuals.

To our daughters

Possibly there is nothing in human nature more resonant with charges than the flow of energy between two biologically alike bodies, one of which has lain in amniotic bliss inside the other.... The materials are here for the deepest mutuality and the most painful estrangement.

—ADRIENNE RICH
Of Woman Born: Motherhood as Experience and Institution

CONTENTS

INTRODUCTION

Motherhood at any age is a daunting proposition. As mothers in our seventies, we know how intimidating it is to look back on all that has taken place with our daughters. We're familiar with the deep mutuality and painful estrangement that has been part of our mothering experience. We review the pleasures, satisfactions, sorrows, and disappointments in these relationships and consider what we might have said or done differently to change the course of events. The mistakes we've made are more apparent to us, the love we have for our daughters feels sharp and strong, and we seek to heal the tensions and misunderstandings that still exist. We are more thoughtful these days, less reactive, and perhaps a bit braver.

Our daughters are among the most important people in our lives, yet they, like us, are changing. They're now middle-aged women with crowded schedules, demanding responsibilities, and multiple commitments. While our lives are contracting and moving toward completion, theirs are expanding, and they are focused on future possibility. The balance between us is shifting; they no longer need us as they once did, and we sometimes find ourselves wanting more from them. More contact. More time. More intimacy.

These grown women are still our children, but we sometimes are uncertain about what mothering feels like, looks like, and means at this stage in our lives. When our daughters were small, our task was to protect, nourish, and guide them, but that is no longer our responsibility. We're aware that we sometimes miss important cues and fail to be sensitive to what they need, or, in our eagerness to be of use, respond with too much advice or frustrate them with unwanted efforts.

Our questions about mothering at this time led us to write this book. We wanted to know more about the challenges and satisfactions of other mothers, the issues that have arisen for them, and the insights they have, thinking that this would help us become clearer about our own experiences of mothering. We also wanted to open a conversation about this extremely important topic because so much misunderstanding exists. Most people assume that mothering is no longer an active role once offspring are solidly in their middle years, yet we are intimately engaged with our daughters in ways that feel like mothering to us. When we asked other aging women if they shared our sense of this ongoing, active role, the vast majority said they did.

Intrigued by the discrepancy between perception and reality, we began to immerse ourselves in what has been written about mothering middle-aged daughters. The words of poets and novelists gave us a glimpse of the language and emotional honesty we wanted, and this encouraged us, but when we turned to nonfiction and psychological research, our search failed to yield results. Most of what has been published about mothering is geared toward younger women with young daughters and contains guidance and advice for solving issues in their relationships. But we were interested in descriptions of experience, not prescriptions for improvement or problem solving. We didn't find anything of interest directed to mothers over sixty-five that offered us this perspective.

Once we became aware of the lack of resources available, we turned to the mothers themselves to learn what we could. We decided to focus on their descriptions of these relationships, knowing that if we interviewed their daughters or others in their families, the book would be at odds with our intention to hear about mothering from their point of view. We understand that no relationship exists in a vacuum, and that both mothers and daughters are connected to sons, husbands, partners, and significant others who affect what happens between them. We also understand that many of the issues that arise between mothers and daughters are exacerbated by a pervasive, amorphous societal misogyny and unreasonable expectations of the experience of mothering. We trusted that these dynamics would be revealed through the words of the women we interviewed.

To begin, we crafted an open-ended questionnaire and reached out through ads, email notices, and word of mouth to women whose ages ranged from sixty-five to eight-five. We were looking for those who are generally active, healthy, and independent enough not to need much financial or emotional care from their daughters at this time. We were committed to including a wide range of class backgrounds, racial identities, ethnicities, sexual orientations, and levels of education, and we chose a mix of working and retired women, as well as those who were single, divorced, lesbian, married, partnered, and living in blended families.

Ultimately, we met with seventy-eight women, most of

whom lived in the San Francisco Bay Area. Our interviews usually took several hours, the physical environments ranged from spacious family homes to small studio apartments, and mothers were uniformly grateful and eager to talk about their daughters in ways they had not done before, except perhaps with a partner, close friend, or therapist. There were tears and hesitations as women searched for the right words to express the complexity of their feelings about mothering these offspring. We heard their pride and concern, their struggles in constructing what felt like appropriate boundaries, and their deep regrets and efforts at forgiveness for both the consequential and unwitting mistakes they had made through the years.

From these interviews we collected a vast amount of material that we supplemented with notes from informal conversations we had with other mothers who were keen to tell us their stories once they heard about our project. We are enormously grateful to all the women who openly shared their life histories and reflections, especially those who invited us into their homes and sat with us during the interviews. We were often surprised and moved by what they said, and their insights and wisdom impressed us. A strength of love and concern for their daughters, even in troubled relationships, was always present. Every woman's story was different and important for us to hear, each voice unique.

As we studied this material, certain themes emerged, providing the scaffolding for the book. Mothers, we discovered, are most interested in talking about the question of closeness with their daughters, puzzling over what creates it or causes a rupture. They search for answers by describing the match between their daughters' and their temperaments and values, and they are aware of how their complicated, unique histories continue to affect their relationships. They mother in a variety of ways—some of which are helpful, others of which can cause problems—and they learn to be sensitive to the shifts in their daughters' needs. Anger, resentment, competitiveness, and envy are common issues that arise and must be navigated as well as possible.

We also learned that mothers are careful what they say to their daughters as a way of protecting themselves against anticipated judgment, disapproval, or rejection, and this self-silencing makes them feel unknown and unseen. Many are fearful of future dependency on their daughters and the loss of their autonomy. At this time in their lives, they're engaged in the process of coming to terms with these relationships as they are now. Some mothers suffer in disappointment about what is missing or unresolved, while others accept the limitations and imperfections of their relationship and grow to hold greater appreciation for their daughters and what they share.

One of the greatest concerns we had in writing this book was to ensure the privacy of the women who confided in us. Mothers did not want their daughters to read more in these pages than they were ready to say directly to them. In order to provide protection to our interviewees, we created six composite mothers who represent the demographic characteristics of those in our study and many of the qualities and relational patterns that emerged. Each has a distinct personality and style of mothering, and their detailed stories are woven throughout. Over the course of the book you will become familiar with Pat, Dolores, Gloria, Margo, Florence, and Cindy, and their complex bonds with their middle-aged daughters.

These composite mothers do not cover the variety of experience of all the women we interviewed, however. So, in order to give a fuller picture, we've supplemented their stories with the words, thoughts, feelings, arrangements, and practices of some of the actual mothers who spoke to us. Their voices are altered to protect their privacy, and their presence gives further witness to the reality that no two women have the same mothering relationships with their middle-aged daughters.

This book is the beginning of a conversation that offers no panaceas, but our hope is that aging mothers will become increasingly aware of the challenges and satisfactions of their relationships and open to talking about them with others. We believe it is important for mothers to acknowledge the complex truths that shape their mothering and recognize the societal expectations that cause them to doubt themselves. We invite readers to find themselves in these pages, reflect on what they read, and add their own insights and questions. There are so many stories that need telling, truths that demand to be revealed, and hard-won choices that deserve to be shared with others who are eager to learn from their lives.

CHAPTER ONE

A Question of Closeness

We ring the bell of a condo in Walnut Creek, a suburb close to San Francisco, and Pat opens the door and invites us in. Her dog, a big black lab, noses around us, then slips away. We settle on the couch in her living room, making ourselves comfortable, and Pat offers us a cup of tea and the sugar cookies she has just baked. Dressed in loose sweat clothes, she's a large woman with fair skin, cropped gray-blonde hair, and an easy, quick smile.

The conversation begins with us asking Pat some basic questions about herself. She tells us that she lives alone and is eighty-one years old, making her the oldest of the six mothers we introduce here. Since her retirement from her job as the bookkeeper of a large construction company, she has been a volunteer at her local Animal Rescue center, working with abused animals and training dogs for people with special needs. Terri, her daughter and only child, is fifty-four and has an apartment a mile away.

With these details in mind, we are ready to move on. "What is your relationship like with Terri?" we ask.

Our question is simple but not easy for mothers to answer. The bond with their daughters is extremely complex and filled with contradictions, and the task of finding the right words to describe it is enormously daunting. The subject, too, is emotionally difficult for many mothers because it raises feelings of yearning and sorrow as well as love and pride.

Pat, however, answers our question in a confident way. "Terri and I are really close," she says.

Her reference to closeness does not surprise us because almost all mothers identify how close or distant they are to their daughters before telling us anything more. Using this language seems to be the easiest way they have to describe their relationships; it's like choosing a point on a scale between one and ten.

But a scale can be deceptive. We know that underneath Pat's claim of closeness, there is a lot to say about the nature of their bond. It exists in the present with all its contradictions and ambivalences, and is shaped by the past—the inevitable accumulation of the decades, the unspoken life under the surface, the historic resentments and unexpressed jealousies, the attachment and love through the years.

We want to learn as much as we can about Pat and her daughter, but we don't push, knowing that she will open up in the hours ahead. Once mothers get beyond their initial reluctance, most of them appreciate the opportunity to talk honestly about these relationships. Some tell us they've never had a conversation like this before, while others say they seldom reveal such truths to others, even to their friends. When they talk about their daughters to most people, they describe them in the best possible light. Mothers have their pride, after all.

We stop for a moment and consider Pat's report of closeness. "What is it like to be really close?" we ask.

"We love each other a lot," she answers.

Most mothers consider love to be a central ingredient in closeness. If it isn't there, the relationship is thought to be in trouble. But love is never a pure feeling, especially in complex familial relationships, and it is often layered with anger, disappointment, and ambivalence. Since it can't be separated out and easily identified, it's not always clear who loves whom, or why, or when.

But Pat seems sure of the love between herself and Terri. "I'm lucky," she says. "I know a lot of mothers who question if they're loved at all, but that bond has always been there with us. Even when we didn't see each other much." Pat pauses and takes a sip of tea. "But it's not only love that makes us close. We trust each other, and that's important too."

Pat is not unusual is saying that trust is also central for intimacy. Trust means knowing that the bond with their daughters will be there no matter what happens, and the deep connection will make it intact through times of misunderstanding and hardship.

But trust, like love, is sometimes amorphous and subject to change. We have spoken to mothers who report that they lost the feeling of trust when their daughters made unexpected cutting remarks or angry gestures. Unsure where their hostility was coming from, they felt vulnerable and began to protect themselves by being careful about what they said and did around them. Trust returned only with honest conversation or the passage of time.

Pat and Terri are very close, but as we'll see, the history of their relationship is far more complicated than it first appears. Like every other mother and daughter, they have had their hard periods. Still, Pat's belief in the solidity of their connection has carried her through, and she exudes a feeling of satisfaction. "Terri is more important to me than anyone else," she tells us. "I've been married and divorced, but she's always been there. I'm grateful for that."

Dolores, another of the mothers we present here, has a very different story to tell us about her relationship with her daughter. We first meet her in her tidy third-floor Oakland apartment, which she shares on weekends with Vince, her long-time significant other. Dolores retired a year ago from her job as a mammography technician and is now the manager of this large apartment building, supervising rentals and maintenance. A slender woman with shiny black hair clasped at the nape of her neck and watchful eyes, she's wearing a yellow blouse that complements her light brown skin. She is sixty-seven years old, the youngest of the mothers we interviewed.

Dolores invites us to sit on her balcony overlooking the garden, and we pile our papers on the little metal table between us. When we ask her to describe her relationship with her daughter, she answers carefully. "Yolanda is my only child, but we're not at all close. She lives in San Antonio, where I grew up, and seldom comes here. I go to see her once or twice a year but don't stay long. She and her husband work hard, and their three kids are in school and busy afterward, and there's only so much cleaning and cooking I can do." She pauses. "Also she and I don't get along."

We have many questions to ask Dolores, but first we assure her that nearly half of the mothers we interview say they aren't very close to their daughters. We want her to know this because mothers so often feel alone and ashamed when their relations are unhappy.

"It seems like everyone gets along great with their daughters except me," Dolores says with a touch of bitterness. "I run into a lot of women who brag about their daughter this, their daughter that. And then there's bragging about the grandchildren . . . I hardly know mine."

We wait a moment for her to continue. "It's discouraging. Yolanda is very close to my mother—she always has been—but she doesn't want to have much to do with me. She and her grandmother live a few miles apart in San Antonio and talk every day while she hardly has anything to say to me."

Dolores's story is not the first we've heard of a triangle where the mother is the odd person out. It's an excruciating situation. In the hours ahead she will tell us what happened in her family and how their relationship got to be this distant, but for now we stay with her unhappiness.

"It must be hard," we say.

"I don't like it," she says, "but that's life. You don't always get what you want."

The Importance of Contact

Mothers remember when their daughters were little and they watched over them, bathed them and brushed their hair, cooked for them and held them close. These little girls felt like an extension of their own bodies, and there never was a question of how close they were. Mother and daughter were tangled together, one entity.

But the primary intimacy began to loosen during adolescence, daughters moving away and into their own lives. Closeness, so carelessly assumed when their girls were young, was no longer a given, and the trajectory was toward separation. Now these daughters are in the middle of their adult lives, and the question of how close they will be is always present. They are still bound together genetically and by their history, yet there is so much that must be navigated.

Mothers tell us that contact with their daughters is the primary way they feel close. Without contact, they are strangers. As Dolores says, "How can I be close to Yolanda when I hardly see her or talk to her?" Yet mothers know only too well that contact is no longer on their own terms as it once was. Their midlife daughters are juggling household responsibilities and work commitments, navigating relationships, and dealing with a multitude of pressures and issues. They're gearing up their domestic and professional lives while their mothers, as aging women, are winding down. The times they can be together, as well as the contact they have through emails, texts, and phone conversations, now depend more on the younger women's availability and interest than on their mothers' needs and desires.

Yet mothers care deeply about how close they are to their daughters and know from experience that successful contact helps to deepen relationships. They look for ways to make this happen. Time is passing, the years ahead are limited, and they feel a certain urgency.

Even Pat, the first mother we introduced who appears to

feel secure in her relationship with Terri, understands the connection between contact and closeness. "Fortunately I see her all the time, but if I didn't, I'd be worried," she tells us. "It's too easy to drift away."

Finding a Way to Connect

Pat goes on to tell us about a friend of hers from her church who is unhappy because her daughter seldom makes time for her anymore. Recently the daughter made plans to drop by after work, but at the last minute she canceled, saying she had to stay at the office to finish a presentation for a meeting. Pat's friend suspects she had received an invitation to do something more exciting that night, like going out for drinks with friends. Apparently this happens often, and she doesn't believe her daughter's excuses anymore. In her mind, their relationship is disintegrating.

After Pat concludes this story, she says, "I'm sorry for my friend. I know how she feels. Terri went through a period of staying away from me, and it was really hard to endure. I'm grateful that's over."

Mothers vary widely in what they expect and desire in the way of contact. Some find great solace in having regular and predictable times with their daughters. They look forward to celebrating the same holidays with them each year, or seeing them every spring or fall, or talking to them at regular intervals. Whatever their arrangement, they feel the relationship is going well if this pattern continues.

A woman we interviewed whose daughter lives 1,200 miles

away feels that their ongoing closeness is sustained because they send each another long catch-up emails every Sunday. Neither of them likes talking on the phone, and they don't manage to see each other very often, but it's especially important to this mother that she can count on hearing from her daughter at least once a week. She tells us she wakes up on Sunday mornings with a sense of anticipation and wellbeing.

Other mothers, however, don't pay much attention to regularity and are comfortable with spontaneity. Their daughters drop by or call when they're in the mood, which might not be for weeks, but they say they like it this way and their daughters do too. There's no pressure to stick to a schedule or routine. But this lack of regularity, which suits them, would cause many mothers to feel insecure or angry.

We have spoken with women who think that closeness means daily contact. Pat tells us about a neighbor of hers who goes running every morning and stops by her daughter's house on the way home. Her daughter is busy feeding her toddler so they don't always visit for long. "It's a habit they have," Pat says. "Like morning coffee. She would miss their visits terribly if her daughter goes back to work, as she might have to do."

Pat's contact with Terri is frequent, as well. Sometimes the two of them will have just a quick hello on the phone, but often it's a shared meal in the evening or a DVD they watch together. She helps her by doing the bookkeeping for her pet grooming business, so they have that project in common, and they communicate daily about financial matters.

But Pat is aware that the intensity of their interaction can change. "I'm seeing Terri more than ever before," she tells us. "She and her woman partner broke up six months ago, and she's still at loose ends trying to figure out her life. She needs me more these days. But before that, during the three years they were together, I saw her mostly on the run. The two of them did their own thing and I did mine."

We ask Pat if she likes the connection the way it is now. "What mother wouldn't?" she answers. "It feels good to be so close. I love that we share the little moments and do so many things together."

This amount of contact suits Pat, but the story is different for some other mothers. The thought of daily visits or frequent calls makes some feel claustrophobic. We heard from one woman who says she loves her daughter, but that doesn't mean she wants to see her very often. Things are fine the way they are. They get together every few months—the daughter lives an hour away—and between visits they seldom call each other or email. She feels connected to her, and she'd be the first one to help her if there were a crisis, but if she had to talk to her every day, she says she'd go crazy.

When Daughters Aren't Available

We notice in our conversations that misunderstandings and hurt feelings easily arise between mothers and daughters around the question of how much contact they are going to have and how regular it is.

Dolores tells us about a time several years ago when she tried to make things better with Yolanda. "I started calling her in San Antonio more often, but she was always too busy to talk and never got back to me. I felt dismissed and finally gave up."

She begins to talk about a friend who also feels pushed away by her daughter. "Part of her problem is that she had a really close relationship with her own mother until she died and always assumed this was how it would be with her daughter. But this daughter, who lives nearby, goes for weeks without reaching out to her and acts like she doesn't care. My friend can hardly bear it. She wanders around her house waiting for the phone to ring, constantly checking her email and obsessing about the situation."

Dolores goes on to say that she's worried about her friend. "I see how torn up she is. I tell her we have to be tough as mothers. You can't make your daughter want to be with you."

The feeling of rejection that Dolores and her friend experience is not unusual, but we've also met women who are more accepting of their daughters' unavailability. Gloria, the third of the mothers we introduce here, reflects this capacity.

Gloria lives in a comfortable ranch-style home in Novato, a town north of San Francisco, with Judy, her partner of twenty-two years, and their three cats. Before her retirement, she was a case worker at the Child Protection Agency, and she now bikes and exercises daily, counsels girls in foster care who want to go to college, and helps people in the neighborhood who need an extra hand or a word of support. A tall woman with deeply tanned skin and spiky brown hair, she's dressed in faded jeans and has an easy manner. Her gray eyes are kind.

As we settle in with Gloria, she tells us that she has two daughters and is closest to the younger one. When we ask her to describe what they do together, she says that unfortunately they don't get to see each other very often. "Kris lives almost two hours away in San Jose and has a stressful job as a software programmer. When she comes home from work, her twelve-year-old son needs her attention—he's on the autism scale—and her husband, too, since he suffers from an immune disorder. On the weekends she's running errands, driving her son around, cleaning the house, cooking for the week ahead. It's a demanding schedule. There's not much time there for visits with me."

"Is that hard for you?" we ask.

"No, because I understand her situation." While Gloria wishes she could see Kris more often than the three or four times a year they manage, she appreciates the burdens the younger woman is carrying and tries to help by not putting pressure on her to be more available. Despite their infrequent contact, she believes that there is a lot of love and goodwill between the two of them. To her, this is being close.

Gloria is unusual in that she doesn't take her daughter's inaccessibility personally and sees it as the result of an impossible schedule rather than a sign of rejection or disregard. Her daughter's life is hard, and she occasionally volunteers to help her out, but when help is not needed, she accepts that. "I have plenty of other things to do," she tells us. "Now that I'm retired, Judy and I travel when she can get away, and there are all my other commitments."

More Than One Daughter

Gloria seems at peace in her relationship with Kris, and she doesn't need to see her very often to feel connected. But when we ask her about her firstborn daughter, Leanne, she grimaces.

"I hardly exist as far as she's concerned. She's like her dad, an upwardly mobile person. She has her own marketing company in Los Angeles, makes a ton of money, and has a lot of possessions. She's in the big leagues." The goodwill and understanding she has for Kris does not transfer to her older daughter, Leanne. Gloria feels rejected by her, and this is an ongoing source of pain. She goes on to tell us that Leanne has always preferred her father. "Even when she was little, she clung to him, and when we got divorced—she was ten—she wanted to be with him more than with me. I let that happen, and by the time she was a teenager, she lived with him most of the time, although Kris stayed with me."

We have spoken with dozens of women who have more than one daughter, and it's emotionally complicated for those who are close to one and distant from the other. As Gloria says, "I've always felt guilty about the difference in my feelings. Aren't mothers supposed to be equally connected to their children? I love them both, sure, but the bond is so much stronger with the one who returns my love."

She goes on to say that she envies women who are close to both of their daughters, even when their personalities and needs are very different. A friend she sometimes bikes with has a daughter living locally, and she helps her out by shopping for her at Costco and taking her dog to the vet when needed. Sometimes the two of them have a cup of coffee together and exchange news, but they mostly visit on the run. Her other daughter lives two states away, and she doesn't see her very often, but when she does, they have long, confidential talks that allow her to glimpse into the heart of her child.

Gloria says different parts of her friend's personality come out with each of these two daughters. She's lighthearted and easily affectionate with the first one, and they laugh a lot together. With the other she is more focused, settling into long conversations about her daughter's worries and concerns.

"My friend is a better mother than I am," Gloria tells us. "She's batting one hundred percent while I'm barely getting fifty."

We answer by telling her about a mother we know who has three daughters. They all have strong, explosive personalities, and it's a three-ring circus with them fighting among themselves as the mother tries to arbitrate. "Thank you, universe, for not giving me that," Gloria says with a smile.

Nearby or Far Away

Many of the women we interviewed do not have daughters living near them. When we first began our research, we wondered how this would affect their relationships since visits, hugs, and outings are obviously more often possible when daughters are close by. But in the end, we've learned that geography doesn't seem to make much difference in how close mothers say they are with their daughters.

Gloria tells us about a woman she knows who hardly saw her daughter when they lived ten miles apart. Perhaps it was because of unresolved issues between them or only a matter of schedule pressures, but whatever the reason, weeks would go by when she wouldn't hear from her. "The mother accepted this as just the way it was although she wished it were different," Gloria says. "But her story has a surprising ending. Her daughter moved to Texas, and they've become closer. They Skype several times a week now, and her daughter confides in her in ways she never did before. She is having problems with her husband, who is an alcoholic and increasingly taking his anger out on her, and she is bewildered by his behavior and doesn't know how to handle the tensions between them. The mother is worried about the situation but happy to be there for her and feels grateful that she confides in her and trusts her."

Some women say they prefer their daughters living at a distance because they are able to have round-the-clock contact with them while staying in their homes. They see their lives up close and participate in their daily routines, and there's more time for long talks that aren't jammed into busy schedules. They feel they get to know them in a more complete way.

We interviewed a woman who makes a yearly trip to Spain to be with her daughter and grandchildren for a month. She tells us that living together that way, plus Skyping in between visits, brings them closer than she ever was with her own mother, who used to live six blocks from her in Florida. This woman's friends feel sorry for her because her daughter is so far away, but it works for them. The only hard thing is saying goodbye when the visit is over.

Some women, however, report having a harder time maintaining a sense of an ongoing relationship when there is geographical distance. They find it painful to move from the intimacy they have with their daughters during their visits to the wrenching sense of separation they experience afterwards. Many describe this process as an emotional rollercoaster. When they are with their daughters, they are close and affectionate, and the connection is deeply satisfying. But after returning home, there can be a bewildering lack of contact. Calls might be brief, emails few, and the door appears to have been shut. Even if they try to explain to their daughters how painful this is for them, the tempo and intensity of contact typically remains unsatisfying and the situation unchanged.

Dolores, like some other mothers, is unhappy that Yolanda lives in San Antonio, so far away. Her story is particularly poignant. "My parents both emigrated from Mexico before I was born. I grew up in a traditional family, the second of five kids," she says. "I was the rebel, the one who didn't fit in. Right after high school I got pregnant with Yolanda, and I married my boyfriend, then divorced him when she was four. He had no job or money, and during that time I worked long hours in low-paying jobs to support us. My mother ended up taking care of Yolanda, and that's how they got to be so close. I just wasn't around."

Dolores goes on to say that she felt increasingly frustrated by her circumstances in San Antonio after the divorce and moved to California with a boyfriend, leaving Yolanda behind with her mom, thinking she would soon send for her. But it took her longer to get established than she expected, and Yolanda was eleven when she finally came to Oakland. "She hated it here," Dolores says. "She missed San Antonio terribly and especially her grandmother. I was strict with her—I didn't want her to get caught up in the life on the streets—and we fought a lot. I sent her back to San Antonio for summers and she never wanted to return, but I insisted. We lasted five years with her going to school in Oakland until I finally gave in and let her move back there for good."

Dolores is haunted by what she sees as the failure of this

relationship. We ask if she thinks it would be different now if she and her daughter lived nearer to each other. "Maybe . . . it would take a lot on both our parts, but that's the only hope. Otherwise, we'll drift along like we are."

We ask her if she would consider relocating to San Antonio, assuming that her daughter will stay there. "I left because I felt hemmed in by my family and their ways," she says. "I did it to survive. Should I give that up now for her? I don't know."

When Contact Changes

Mother and daughter relationships are like a dance. The partners move toward each other and away, in and out, around and about. Some movements are wild and abrupt while others are more carefully attuned. Over the years the rhythm changes, but one thing is certain: the dance continues to the end.

The rhythm may shift when one of the dancers (usually the daughter) signals that she wants to be less connected. Phone calls and emails are not answered or visits are canceled. There are subtle nonverbal cues: a kiss brushed aside, a vague unavailability. Some mothers are quick to sense that their daughters want more distance. The question, then, is how to respond. A few mothers directly ask their daughters what's going on, but more often than not, they retreat in anger, hurt, or confusion.

We ask Gloria to tell us more about the dance between herself and Leanne, her oldest daughter. "As I said, we've never been very close—but it was better between us about fifteen years ago. She was in her late thirties when she moved to Los Angeles to set up her marketing company, and I used to drive down there a few times a year for a long weekend. We enjoyed going for hikes and movies, hanging out together. But then about five years ago, we were supposed to go to the desert for a weekend, and she canceled at the last minute. When I asked why, I never got a real explanation. I would have understood if she'd had a new romance or an important meeting, but she said it was nothing like that, she just didn't want to go. In the following months, she was always too busy for me to come down there. She had crossed me off her list, or so it seemed. I gave her the space she seemed to want, but it was hard not to take it personally."

Gloria goes on to say that the worst moment came when she found out that Leanne had been in the Bay Area to visit her father a few months after the canceled weekend but hadn't even let her know. "I was really pissed. I ranted around the house for a long time, saying I never wanted to see her again, but Judy, who has a lot more equanimity than I do about this kind of thing, talked me down. Which was good because Leanne finally called—it was a whole year after the canceled desert trip—acting like nothing had happened. She said she was coming up to San Francisco on business, and would I like to meet for dinner at her hotel?"

Gloria is a person who speaks her mind, but she held back during that first meeting with Leanne. "There she was, my firstborn child, dressed in a chic business suit in this classy hotel, and there I sat, wearing my usual jeans and a sweater. We had drinks together and made small talk, mostly about her work. I wanted to grab her or shake her, asking her why she'd cut me off so precipitously—but that would have ruined the opportunity to reconnect. The dinner ended, and I went home having learned nothing about why the falling out between us had happened. But as I told Judy later, a little bit of her is better than none." Since that time Gloria sees Leanne once or twice a year for dinner when she is in town, and otherwise there is not much contact. "Am I angry about this?" she asks. "Absolutely. And, yes, I am also sad. But what can I do?"

Mothers and daughters come together and separate, each pair in their own way. The rhythm changes when one of the partners wants more distance, but it can also shift if one—usually the mother—wants more contact and makes a concentrated effort.

Sometimes mothers act to become closer to their daughters by inviting them to be together more often or asking them to schedule regular contact. If they are fortunate, the daughters are open to these overtures. But some experience this approach as too much pressure and pull further away, leaving their mothers to blame themselves for creating a break in connection that wasn't there before. They tell us they resent that the rhythm of their intimacy depends entirely on their daughters' desires and say this feels unfair and hurtful.

When Closeness Is Missing

One of the greatest heartaches experienced by older mothers is the loss of their daughters through withdrawal or outright rejection. When this happens, their first response is often to search for reasons and try to make sense of the rupture.

We interviewed a woman whose daughter has cut her off for over a year. At first the mother thought this was because she's so involved in her new job, but now the issue seems to be deeper than that. The daughter has been in psychotherapy, and she is convinced the woman therapist is poisoning their relationship. The therapist, she posits, has become the "good" mother while she is now the "bad" mother who caused all her problems. She talks about the therapist seducing her daughter away from her and how unethical that is. When we ask her if she knows this is happening for sure, she looks uncertain for a moment and then says it's the only scenario that makes sense. She and her daughter have had issues in the past, she says, but nothing that would cause this.

Sometimes the estrangement goes on for years. Gloria tells us about a neighbor whose daughter refuses to see her and acts as though she were dead. "I don't know what caused it, but the situation has been going on for twenty years. Her daughter lives in Boston with her husband and a grown son whom this woman has never been allowed to meet. It's a great sorrow." Gloria says that she and Judy invite their neighbor over for dinner every so often to keep her spirits up. "She lives alone— apparently there was a second marriage that went sour—and she gets into a terrible state of anxiety. We watch out for her." When we ask Gloria if she thinks there's anything that can be done to heal this split, she shakes her head. "Through the years she tried to contact her daughter, but letters were returned, the phone slammed down, gifts sent back unopened, and pleas from friends who tried to intervene were unanswered. This woman even went to Boston and appeared at her front door but was turned away. Short of kidnapping her daughter, she's tried everything."

Other more fortunate mothers have managed to reclaim relationships that have been broken. One respondent went through a painful period when her daughter refused to see her, demanding a complete separation to sort out her life and her feelings. While she understood why she would want this, at least in theory, she could hardly bear the excruciating and extended silence that followed. She felt certain the two of them could work through whatever had gone wrong between them, but she had to wait for nearly two years before her daughter let her know that she was ready to see her again.

When they were finally able to talk together, she was able to sit quietly and listen to her daughter's feelings without defensiveness, something that's hard for her to do. She's come to understand that her natural sense of authority makes her daughter feel insecure about her own capabilities, and she now realizes that she needs to support her as she is without giving her suggestions for improvement. The mother feels grateful for the opportunity to recalibrate their relationship and has asked her daughter to tell her when she slips up, as she knows she inevitably will. She is, after all, used to being confident and in control.

Some Mothers Want Less Contact

Pat, Dolores, and Gloria, like most other mothers, have a strong desire to be connected to their daughters. They feel satisfied if their relationships fall within the parameters of what they call closeness and dissatisfied if they don't. At the base of this is their assumption that a certain amount of contact is important in making a successful relationship. As Gloria says, "It's like greasing the wheels."

Mothers generally seem to be more invested in having a close relationship than do their middle-aged daughters, who tend to be less available and sometimes less interested. But we have met a few women who tell us that they already have too much contact with their daughters and wish they could have less. They describe them as needy and troubled, a drain on their energy and resources, and they feel depleted by these relationships.

Margo, the fourth mother we include here, expresses these feelings. We first meet her in the spacious brown-shingle home in the Berkeley hills that she shares with Ted, her husband. She's a bright-eyed woman with olive skin, a wreath of silver curls floating around her head, and a large, expressive mouth, and she seems to be in constant motion, shifting in her armchair, fingering the necklace around her neck, pulling at one strand of hair and then another. She tells us that she and Ted raised two children, a daughter and a son, in this house. The setting, with the surrounding redwood trees, is idyllic, and so is Margo's life in many ways. "Except," she tells us, "for my daughter, Elise."

Behind Margo's house is a small cottage where Elise, a single mom, has lived for the past five years. When we ask Margo to describe their relationship, she says they are close in some ways but not in others. "She's right under my nose all the time. I suppose that's being close. But she's depressed and hardly functioning, and we don't have much of an adult relationship. She sits there inside that cottage most days, feeling self-critical, and then she knocks on my kitchen door and wants to complain about everything. I feel like yelling at her to go away and figure out her own life. I have lots of other commitments and things I want to do. Maybe I'm being selfish, but I've paid my dues as a mother, and I just don't want the job any longer. I feel guilty, of course, and tell myself to be more compassionate. My daughter can't help who she is, and she needs my support. Where else can she turn?"

Added to Margo's distress is the fact that she's a psychotherapist, still seeing ten clients a week. "You'd think I could deal with this situation better. I work with emotionally disturbed people in my practice all day long, but having one in my own family is another matter." She tells us that Elise has a lot of internalized rage, and it gets directed at her. "It's a no-win situation. Yesterday Elise was complaining about the fifteen pounds she's gained this past year, and I suggested it could be her meds and she should check that out with her doctor. She exploded, saying I always try to tell her what to do. I apologized and walked away, but I was seething. Elise is passive-aggressive—she set me up by telling me about her weight and I took the bait by giving her advice." Margo pauses for a minute. "If I were being honest with her, I would have told her she should stop stuffing her face with junk food and get out of the house and exercise, and then she would be thinner. But that would be really hurtful."

Living in such close proximity to Elise is a strain for Margo, who was born Jewish but has adopted a Buddhist spiritual practice. "This situation with my daughter forces me to look at my impatience and my lack of empathy. It's part of my spiritual work," she tells us. "In theory I welcome it and I've grown from it, but truthfully, I wish Elise and her problems would just go away."

Becoming a Grandmother

The one good thing for Margo about her daughter living in her backyard is that she gets to see her ten-year-old grandson every day. "Ted and I are crazy about him," she says with a smile. "He's so bright and funny. He must take after his Columbian dad whom we've never met, but we've been told he's an engaging, warm man."

Margo loves to be around children because it reminds her of when her own were little, and she played games and did art projects with them. "The only downside is that I don't really share this pleasure with Elise. Her son feels like a burden to her, and she doesn't know how to enjoy him."

Margo has not become closer to Elise through being a grandmother, but she tells us about a friend who has had the opposite experience. "I'm so envious. In the past my friend and her daughter didn't have much to say to each other, but that's changed. She's always been included in her daughter's family life and told everything that goes on with the grandkids. The oldest one is applying to college this month, and my friend's right in the middle of that drama, very excited about the possibilities. She says her daughter seems to understand and respect her more now that she herself has experienced the stresses and strains of raising kids. It's great for her that she's receiving so much affirmation. Lucky woman."

One common assumption is that becoming a grandmother will foster closeness between mothers and their daughters because they now have a grandchild in common. As a culture we cherish the image of the involved grandma, the older woman who takes care of the kids and brings warmth and comfort to her daughter's home. This is true for Margo's friend and many other women, but it doesn't happen that way for everyone. Dolores tells us that her grandchildren haven't brought her any closer to Yolanda. "On one of my last trips to San Antonio, I tried to get to know the kids better and hoped that would help to smooth things over with my daughter. I brought them presents, and they liked that, but I don't know anything about Minecraft and those other computer games the two boys play, and my granddaughter texted and stayed online the whole time. They hardly talked to me. The kids have a lot of relatives in town, all those aunts, uncles, and cousins on both Yolanda's and her husband's sides, and I was just one more who happened to be there for a short visit. They were polite—I give Yolanda that—but they weren't at all interested in me."

Grandchildren are one of life's greatest pleasures, many women say. But their existence sometimes creates a feeling of distance from daughters who are preoccupied with parenting and not as available as they were before. Gone are the days of lively discussion about issues outside the small concerns of family life, and mothers can feel disappointed about how narrow their daughters' interests have become, even though they understand the demands of childrearing. Sometimes they report a feeling of envy for the attention and affection the children get from their daughters and wish that some of it were directed their way.

We've spoken with women who find that their dreams of closeness with their daughters don't materialize, but they're deeply connected to their grandkids instead. One mother lives in the back room of a house her daughter and husband bought a year ago, and she sees her daughter only in passing and never alone. The care of her two grandkids and the household cooking are on her shoulders while their parents go off to work. She thinks the only reason her daughter invited her to move in with them was to be a babysitter and a maid, and this angers her. She has considered moving out but has become attached to her grandchildren and wants to be around to provide them with a calm daily structure. She's given up trying to deepen her relationship with her daughter.

It is not possible to predict how the presence of grandchildren will affect mothers' relationships with their daughters. Some say the best time is when their first grandchild is born.

Gloria tells us, "When Kris, my youngest, had her son, I was able to take two weeks off from work to be with her. She was pretty freaked out—she'd hardly been around babies before, and she was intimidated by breastfeeding and changing diapers. It had been a long time since I did all that, but you never really forget, and suddenly I was the expert. She probably could have figured out these things by herself, but I made it easier for her. I got a lot of gold stars for that!"

Many mothers tell us that their daughters feel vulnerable and unsure of themselves with this first birth and consequently more accepting of their help and expertise than they have been in years. This creates a deep connection between them. When the second child is born, the level of intensity usually is not repeated; mothers might be called upon to help, but now there is an older brother or sister running around, needing attention, and their daughters already know about infant care and don't need their guidance anymore. Still, their presence is appreciated, and mothers treasure these experiences.

Different Ways of Being Close

Closeness between mothers and daughters comes about in a variety of ways. There are those that involve a planned activity, like getting together to celebrate a birthday or going camping together, and those that are unstructured or spontaneous, like dropping by for a cup of coffee or a phone call just to say hello. Most mothers say they have both kinds of experiences with their daughters, although some seem to be most comfortable with one kind or the other, depending on their personalities and their relationships.

Mothers frequently tell us that shopping is their favorite way of being together. As Pat says, "Even though I see Terri almost every day at her pet grooming salon or after work, it's still something very special when we go to the mall together. We leave behind our worries, and we're on an adventure, with the main goal of enjoying ourselves. It doesn't even matter if we buy something. I watch her try on clothes—she has the same broad back and narrow waist I had when I was her age, before I got so heavy—and I have a feeling of history. I see before me my grandmother, my mother, me, and now Terri, all of us with the same youthful body."

Shopping sometimes brings unexpected intimacy, as one mother told us. She was in a department store with her daughter recently and they wandered through the children's clothing department on their way to the escalator. Suddenly her daughter began to weep. The mother took her in her arms and cradled her, something she had not done for twenty years, and afterward her daughter told her how discouraged she was that she hadn't gotten pregnant that month after a year of trying. It was a sad but intimate afternoon.

Sharing meals is also a way that women connect with their daughters. It can be grabbing an unexpected bite together during the daughter's lunch break. Or bringing over a pot of chicken soup when her daughter is sick. Or going out to eat at a favorite place. One mother says she researches the best restaurants in Chicago before she flies there to visit her daughter, and she invites her to a special dinner, just the two of them.

Food plays a central role in the life of mothers and daughters, binding together the past and the present. Mothers tell us about the simple and companionable pleasure of chopping vegetables, cooking pasta sauce, or baking a chocolate cake with their daughters. For one, it's creating tamales, as she learned to do from her own mother when she was little, and for another, it's making dolmas every year before Christmas with her two daughters and grandchildren, an all-day affair of singing, talking, and teasing each other, their way of being close.

Cooking has a deep emotional resonance in women's and daughters' lives. Making, serving, and eating food is the way many families express love. The recipes that are handed down through the generations are treasured, and the pleasures about this shared heritage reverberate in the present. Holidays, especially, bring forth memories about special food and are often a way mothers and daughters find each other in the midst of their busy lives.

Margo tells us that her best times with Elise are centered on food. "When Hanukkah comes, we really celebrate," she says. "She rises to the occasion, and we make latkes and applesauce together, like we did when she was little. We talk about her grandma, whom we used to call *bubbe,* and how she loved this holiday. Then in the evening, my son and his partner come over and Ted and my grandson are here, too, and we light the Hanukkah candles and have a great feast. It feels like we're one happy family at that time."

Cooking and shopping are the two most often-mentioned shared activities that bring a sense of closeness that many women long for with their daughters. But women are creative and find other ways to sustain this connection. Margo tells us about her tennis partner who carves out private time with her overworked daughter one Sunday each month. "The two of them meet at the head of a nearby trail at seven a.m. and hike together among those gorgeous redwoods," she says. "It's a really special time for her. She hates to get up early in the morning and wouldn't do it for anyone but her daughter."

Margo also tells us about a neighbor of hers who was thrilled when her daughter became interested in her work as a quilter and took some introductory quilt-making classes. After learning the basics, her daughter began to create quilted collages out of her children's old clothes and baby blankets. Now the two of them talk about quilt stitches and patterns, and they are at their closest when they share their work. "They have discovered a new language," Margo says. "On the surface they're discussing technical details, but underneath is a sense of sharing something deeply personal and precious about creativity. This has brought the two of them together."

Many mothers experience closeness through shared activities with their daughters, but others might not have the time or the interest to engage in this way, or they seldom see each other, or it's just not their habit.

Sometimes the bedrock of intimacy rests in the level of honesty and self-disclosure in conversations. A colleague talked about being raised in what she describes as an emotionally autistic family, and the fact that she is able to create a satisfying level of intimacy with her daughter through language is a source of enormous pride. It gives her the sense of connection she yearned for herself as a daughter. She describes how she recently told her daughter about the questions she's been asking as she approaches her seventy-fifth birthday, reflecting on her shifting priorities, her diminishing capacities, and the unexpected freedom she feels with aging. Her daughter responded by saying that she, at fifty-five, is asking the same questions, although her answers are different. The very fact that they were having such a parallel yet distinct conversation was thrilling to her.

Other mothers speak of the satisfaction they feel when their daughters confide in them. It's those moments of verbal intimacy and understanding that mean the most.

Gloria describes what happened when she last visited Kris in San Jose. "I drove there for her forty-ninth birthday, and we had a little party with Indian food and birthday cake. When I was ready to leave, she slipped into the car next to me. Neither of us is a big talker about things that bother us, so I was surprised when she blurted out that her husband and son were causing her grief and there were just too many demands on her. 'Maybe I'll come home with you,' she said in a half-joking way. I told her I'd love that and there's always a place for her in Judy's and my home. She thought for a moment, then replied that such a thing was impossible, her family needed her. I didn't say much, only that I was sorry it was so hard, but I reached out and squeezed her hand. Afterwards, as I drove the long freeway home, I felt like part of me was still there, holding her hand."

Words are the path to closeness for some mothers, but others say they are most intimate in silent ways. Margo told us that her cousin and her daughter are physically affectionate. That's their language of love. For them, touching is equal to all the words in the world.

"You can see it when you're with them," Margo says. "They never sit far apart on the couch, like Elise and I do. They touch lightly or stroke each other as they pass by, and they drape around each other. It's beautiful that two adult women, both of them with full, functional lives, are so physically connected. I wish it were that way with Elise and me. When she was little, I touched her a lot, but she started resisting it when she was a teenager and that was the end. It makes me sad."

Contact without words can be a form of intimacy. We spoke with another mother who says she knows she is loved simply by the way her daughter looks at her. The feeling of their special connection is there in her eyes, without words, and she doesn't need anything more than that to feel close. For her, the amount or nature of their contact isn't nearly as important as this private, nonverbal expression of their bond.

Comparing Relationships

On the most obvious level, mothers rate how well they're doing with their daughters by how the connection feels to them. But that isn't the end of the story. They inevitably compare their relationships to those of other mothers and daughters.

We spoke with many women who grew up in large, extended families that immigrated to the United States from China, Eastern Europe, and Latin America. They saw their own mothers in constant contact with their grandmothers and aunts, shopping, cooking, and caring for the children. Now, when they compare their relationships with their adult daughters to what they witnessed in the past, they conclude they are failing.

Dolores tells us about her family. "My grandmother, my *abuela*, lived with us during my childhood, and she and my mom did everything together. Sure, they quarreled sometimes, but it didn't matter. I grew up thinking this was how mothers and daughters were supposed to be. My sisters are still like that with my mother, though they live in separate houses, but here I am, cut off from family, hardly talking to my daughter. I can't help but judge myself."

Margo's family also immigrated to the States, settling in New Jersey after arriving from Poland in 1926. As she tells us, "My grandparents lived in the apartment above us, and my *bubbe* and my mother went up and down those stairs all day long, talking about what to buy at the greengrocer's, whether to go to the doctor, or the latest gossip in the neighborhood. Nobody thought that was unusual; it was just how life was. When I moved twenty miles away, after Ted and I got married, it was as though I had crossed the ocean, but I still visited a few times a week, carting along my two little kids. If I didn't, I felt guilty."

Margo goes on to say that it's ironic how things have turned out with Elise. "She lives here, and in my family's eyes, that would be considered how it's supposed to be. But we hardly talk, and they would never understand that. We've failed when I compare our relationship to what my mother and my grandmother had. I have to work really hard not to blame myself or be angry with her. My meditation practice helps me with this, but the feelings keep coming up."

It isn't only the children of immigrant families who compare their current relationships to what they witnessed as children. Just about every mother we've interviewed does this, whatever her family background. Some, like Margo, have glowing memories of how things were between their mothers and grandmothers, but other families were not as loving. Or even tolerable. Women describe relationships they witnessed between their mothers and grandmothers that were estranged or abusive, and have worked hard to avoid that in their own lives.

Pat remembers, "My grandma was really crazy. She lashed out often at my mom, who stayed away from her as much as she could. That's what I grew up seeing. My mom, fortunately, wasn't so mean to me, but she wasn't very demonstrative or caring either. She was wounded as a child and never got over it. I always knew I wanted to be a different kind of mother, and when Terri was born, I was overcome with love for this tiny creature who depended so much on me. I did my best, and I can say we're really close. Sometimes I can hardly believe my good fortune."

Other women, however, say they are distrustful about the possibility of closeness with their daughters because of their own personal histories. They assume there's always going to be heartache and friction because that's how it has been through the generations in their families. The reasons for this, they say, are jealousy, competition, and different personalities bumping up against each other, and nothing can be done to change this reality.

Family experience is central in determining how mothers think about closeness and how they judge themselves. But they don't live in a vacuum, and equally important is the comparison they make with friends and others they know or hear about.

Over the years, Margo has worked with dozens of older mothers in her psychotherapy practice and heard many stories about parenting. "I have to admit that when I hear a client talk about her relationship to her daughter, a tiny part of me is comparing myself to her. This last week I saw a woman who was suffering because of her estrangement from her daughter, and as I listened, there was a little voice inside me saying, 'See, Margo, you don't have it so bad. Compared to her, you and Elise are doing pretty good. There's a lot to complain about, but you muddle through and love each other underneath it all.' I'd never say anything to my client about what I was thinking, and I feel embarrassed to admit these thoughts to you, but that's the truth."

The weight of comparison cannot be underestimated. Mothers tend to feel most comfortable if their relationships with their daughters are similar to those of their friends or others they know. They sense the existence of unspoken norms about the amount of contact that should take place: any less is worrisome, and any more would be too much.

Margo tells us that she sometimes feels judged because she allows Elise to live in the cottage. One friend recently insisted that it's an unhealthy situation and she should consider asking her daughter to leave. "She's right that I'm stressed out, and

Elise is, too," Margo says. "But the problem isn't that she lives here. I'm a firm believer in multigenerational living arrangements because they can be good for everyone. The problem is her lack of functioning and us being at odds with each other. If those things were different, I'd love to have her in and out of my house every day. It worked for my mom and my *bubbe*. I'm a gregarious person and want my family around me."

Mothers evaluate themselves in a multitude of ways. They even compare their relationships with their daughters to what they see in the media or read in books. Margo, an inveterate reader, recently began a highly recommended novel about the love and struggles of a mother and daughter, but she put it down after a while because she realized it just made her feel more depressed. She and Elise are far from loving each other in the open, sensitive way described in the book, and she doesn't see a way forward.

Mothers' Yearning

In talking with mothers, we are struck again and again with their strong yearning to be close to their daughters at this time in their lives. Those who are close say they consider themselves to be fortunate, lucky, or blessed. It's a reason for celebration and gratitude, and they are proud of what they've accomplished and think of it as a significant achievement. However, when a serious breach exists, there is "a hole," as one mother calls it, and sometimes it is seen as "even worse than death." These women suffer from the loss of their daughters and say they long for repair and closeness.

Relationships are never static, however, and mothers know that closeness can fade, even if blood binds. They've heard stories about daughters who disappear from contact or are swayed in another direction by a hostile new partner. Or a relationship that comes unraveled because of an ugly family blowup or is shattered by the emergence of a previously unexpressed, ancient anger. Far in the background in most mothers' minds—even those who are very close to their daughters—is the fear that this relationship, this one that is so precious to them, might change in a direction that will cause discontinuity and sorrow.

Mothers who are currently distant from their daughters continue to have the hope that there will be a change that will bring them back into contact. No matter how fractured their relationship, no matter how discouraging the separation may be, mothers continue to hold the dream that there will be a healing. They imagine the scenario and play it out in their minds. The time might be far off, and the reconciliation might not be all they wish for, but reconnection might happen if only the right words are said, if only the hardness of heart dissolves, if only there is forgiveness. Every mother with a troubled relationship has this hope, no matter how many years have elapsed or how hard she has tried to convince herself to accept her daughter's alienation as a fact of life.

Being a mother at any age is a precipitous task, perhaps even more so when a woman is in her later years, looking back over the course of her life and focusing on the state of her relationship with her daughter. If their bond is strong, there is a desire to preserve what they have, and if there is tension, to resolve it. Mothers want things settled. Time is short. No longer is there a hazy span of years opening to the future, and this realization brings a sense of urgency.

Yet living with this sense of urgency is too disruptive, and they have the impulse to push away these disturbing thoughts. The concerns of everyday life take precedence. Schedules must be kept, calls made, obligations fulfilled. Their relationships with their daughters slip into a familiar perspective, and life goes on in its confounding, unpredictable way.

CHAPTER TWO

Generation to Generation

During our interviews we ask mothers why they think their relationships with their daughters have turned out to be as they are. Most say that the basic similarities and differences between them play an extremely important role. This explanation sounds promising, but in reality it does not lead us to any conclusions because each mother-daughter pair is unique. One mother may be convinced that she and her daughter get along well because they are so similar, but another tells us that they are at odds because they're too much alike. Or one woman says that she has trouble with her daughter because they're so different, while another insists they are attached precisely because of their differences. The confusion about similarities and differences grows even greater for mothers who have more than one daughter.

After hearing dozens of explanations, we can only say that what works well for one mother and daughter might well be a problem for another. Still, we find it fascinating that mothers give so much importance to the fit of similarities and differences as they try to make sense of the confusing state of their relationships.

Cindy, who is seventy years old and the fifth mother we include here, is highly conscious of the differences between herself and her daughter, Frida. We first meet her in her artist's studio behind the house she's renting on an apple farm in Petaluma, north of San Francisco. A small woman with pale, freckled skin and long, auburn-gray hair wrapped around her head, she apologizes for the cluttered state of her studio. "It's a horrible mess," she says. "I keep meaning to tidy it up." She clears off a paint-spattered bench so we can sit down. "I'm a mixed media artist," she tells us. "But Frida, my daughter, thinks that's just an excuse for me to hoard a lot of stuff. I suppose she's right. I can never throw anything out."

We notice a six-foot installation on the wall made with swatches of colorful fabric, yarn, and artfully arranged sticks, and we observe how striking it is. Cindy tells us she hopes to sell it to a large corporation that is opening its general office in the area. "Frida says I'm foolish to think they'll be interested in it," she says with a smile, "but you never know. I'm an optimist."

Cindy goes on to describe her daughter. "She's not at all like me. She's practical and realistic, a successful partner at her San Francisco law firm. I named her Frida, after the great artist Frida Kahlo, but she doesn't have an artistic bone in her body. I admire her because she's so organized and manages so much, including her two teenaged kids. I could never be like her because my mind doesn't work in that systematic, logical way. I'm a dreamer."

"Is it hard having a child who is so different?" we ask.

"Not now," she answers. "But when she was younger, we fought all the time. She hated the way I was and the chaos I brought into her life. After high school she moved out and worked her way through college and law school, and we were like strangers. Then about ten years ago I moved here to Petaluma and she was also living in the Bay Area, so we began to see each other once in a while. Finally we were able to talk about what had happened in her childhood. She told me how angry she was about how I'd been as a mother, and I assured her she was absolutely right, I had been terribly irresponsible. I apologized to her with my whole heart."

"How is it with the two of you now?" we ask.

"Compared to how it was before, we're pretty close."

When Cindy names the differences between herself and Frida, she is talking about their temperaments. She's free-spirited, artistic, and creative, and Frida is linear, logical, and careful. She thinks of them as opposites, and the reason they are "pretty close" now is that they have made progress in accepting each other's differences. As Cindy says, "We're stuck with each other. She's my only child, and I'm her only parent since her dad lives in England. If we don't find a way to get along, we both lose."

When mothers talk about similarities and differences, they most often are referring to temperament. They might call it by another name—personality, nature, or disposition—but they consider it to be a given, like the color of their eyes or the shape of their hands. The interplay between their daughter's and their temperaments, they say, is at least partly the reason they are drawn to each other or struggle with what seem to be insurmountable obstacles.

Mothers and Daughters with Different Temperaments

~∾~

Cindy and Frida have a hard time finding common ground because of their temperamental differences. "I'm good at reading people, but no matter how hard I try, I usually can't figure her out," Cindy says. "A while back I called to say hi—it had been over a month—and she sounded angry, her voice all knotted up and tight, and I thought, *Oh no, what did I do wrong now?* But it turned out she had been going over a law case when I phoned and she was preoccupied. It had nothing to do with me. If she hadn't said something about having so many cases to review that evening, I would have made the wrong assumption and taken her coldness personally."

Mothers keep coming back to the existence of temperamental similarities and differences when they try to explain the difficulties in their relationships. Gloria, like Cindy, has to stretch her mind to understand her older daughter, Leanne. "We speak different languages," she tells us. "She's an ambitious woman with a discerning eye, and she judges and rejects those things that don't meet her standards. There's a hardness in her that surprises me again and again."

Gloria is anything but hard herself. For thirty years, before she retired, she worked at an agency for kids who were being abused or maltreated. She can be a little brusque, but underneath this exterior is a tender heart. "I don't think Leanne cares about much of anything except to get ahead," she says. "If she saw a dog get hit by a car, I doubt she'd stop if she were going to an important business meeting."

She goes on to tell us that she thinks she and Leanne have completely different temperaments. "She's ambitious, and I'm not. She likes to be in charge, and I don't. She craves possessions, and I could care less. She's goal-driven, and I've never had any. She's impatient, and I take my time. She's quick to draw conclusions, and I try to see all sides of things."

We ask Gloria if there are any ways she and daughter are alike, given these obvious differences. "I'm sure there are," she answers, "but I can't think of them."

"What about relating to people?" we ask.

She stops for a minute. "I suppose she's a mix of extroversion and introversion, and that's like me. We both get along with people but are also okay being alone. That's probably the only thing we have in common."

Gloria tells us she has never thought about this similarity before. "How did I miss it?" she wonders. "I'm usually the one who is really aware of where people fall on the introversion–extroversion scale. I was talking this morning with a woman I know who calls herself a "people's person," and she loves to sit and talk with friends, hang out in groups, organize social events. She's a great extrovert, but her daughter is shy and retiring, and shuns people. It's no surprise that those two have big problems. The mother was saying today that she's tearing her hair out because whenever she talks to her daughter, there is hardly any response. She doesn't think her daughter is hostile or depressed; it's just the way she is, and she has concluded they can never be truly close because of this vast difference between them. I told her I know how she feels because of my issues with Leanne."

Temperamental differences can cause some women to feel

inadequate with their daughters. Cindy is sure that Frida looks down on her because of how "untogether" she is. "I'm messy and disorganized," she says gesturing around her art studio. "That's pretty obvious. I really respect Frida—I think she's amazing—but that respect is not returned. It really hurts my feelings and makes me feel like a failure. She hardly ever comes here, but recently she dropped by unexpectedly when she was driving back on the interstate after meeting with a client further north. I was thrilled to see her, but I could tell by her pinched expression how disgusted she was by the state my house was in. True, it was pretty bad. The kitchen table was covered with unopened mail and used takeout containers, the cats' litter box was overflowing, and dirty dishes were piled in the sink. She didn't stay long, and when she left I collapsed on my bed and wept. Once again I had failed to be the kind of person my daughter could respect and admire."

Cindy suffers from Frida's judgment of her temperament and thinks they'll never be able to connect more intimately because of their differences. But differences can lead to closeness for some mothers. They value these distinctions and wouldn't have their daughters be any other way.

Cindy tells us about a ceramic artist friend of hers who appreciates her daughter's calm nature. "This woman has suffered from anxiety all her life," she says. "Medication has helped, but her feeling of panic is still just below the surface. Her daughter, who is temporarily living with her, is more easygoing and doesn't have the same fears or phobias. She quiets her mother down and distracts her when she gets tense by telling her funny stories. The mother is grateful to have a daughter with a more relaxed temperament than hers and likes to think that the women in her family are getting better through the generations. She has surpassed her own mother, who was completely incapacitated by fear and couldn't leave the house, and now her daughter has exceeded her and does not suffer at all from anxiety." Cindy stops. "It's a nice story, isn't it? I wish it was like that with Frida and me. But Frida is judgmental of the way I am, and this woman's daughter accepts her as she is, and that's a huge difference."

Some mothers feel that their daughters' temperaments heighten their connection rather than diminish it. One woman described her daughter as a warm, generous person who brings out the best in everyone around her. People flourish in her presence, including her. She is private, shy, and more introverted, and doesn't connect to others with the ease and concern her daughter has. She shakes her head in wonder that she has been so fortunate to have a daughter with such a loving, kind nature and says she is constantly learning from her.

When Mothers and Daughters Have Similar Temperaments

Many women dream of having daughters like themselves, intimate beings with similar natures. Pat says that she is fortunate because Terri's and her minds work the same way. "We know what each other means before the words pop out of our mouth," she tells us. "We're alike in how we approach tasks. Yesterday there was a problem at Terri's shop when a client claimed that her dog had not received the full treatment that had been arranged. She handled it exactly as I would have, explaining what happened in a reasonable, good-natured way, working it out without getting upset or reactive. We're both like that, and it makes getting along so easy."

Some lucky mothers have the symmetry of temperament with their daughters that Pat describes. It creates a deep sense of attunement for them, and they say that it's the bedrock upon which their relationship rests.

Margo describes the yearning she has had for this kind of fit with Elise through the years. "I suppose it's narcissistic, but I would just love it if she were more like me. Even when she was little, I kept looking for signs, but they were few and far between. If we were more alike, I think we'd be able to understand each other a whole lot better and our relationship would improve."

Margo talks about one of her therapist friends who has a very close connection with her daughter. "They notice the same kinds of things—a lovely rock, the shape of a tree branch, the rise of a shoulder. They're hooked into each other because they are so much alike. They can sense each other's mood shifts and read each other's facial expressions, and there's an energetic pull between them. When I'm in their presence, I can feel it. Of course there are things about them that are different, but fundamentally, they have always been on the same wavelength."

Margo continues to describe this relationship but then stops herself. "I shouldn't idealize what my friend has," she says. "I've been around long enough to know that sameness doesn't always mean closeness. Plenty of mothers say it's a curse, not a blessing."

In our interviews, we too have heard many stories about the difficulties mothers and daughters have because of their similarities. Dolores describes how this dynamic has played out with Yolanda. "It took me a long time to see it, but she and I are not that different from each other. She's stubborn, just like I am. She clings to what she thinks is right, and she rejects something if it doesn't fit. I'm the same way. Even though we hardly talk, even though we don't see each other often, there is this feeling of a tug of war, each of us obstinately holding on to who we are."

We ask Dolores if she thinks this could be resolved. "I doubt it. We're both too set in our ways."

She tells us about a friend in her apartment building who also doesn't get along with her daughter. They both have big tempers, and when the mother travels to stay with her, as she does at Christmas each year, they last about three days before fighting erupts. Many times she returns home early because the atmosphere becomes too tense and uncomfortable. Dolores says that both of them are hotheaded, and although they love each other, they can hardly be together because they share such a volatile temperament.

When we ask Dolores what she thinks about this, she says that mothers and daughters are lucky if they're alike in good ways, like being patient or kind. "But if they're alike in not-so-good ways, like being stubborn or getting angry easily, it's double trouble."

Echoes from the Past

Many mothers have told us that their daughters remind them of people who hurt or abused them in the past. When this likeness exists, they find that it is difficult to see them just as themselves and to separate them from that historic pain.

Gloria has struggled with the ways Leanne is like her ex-husband. "Not only does she look like him—the same coal black hair and jutting chin—but she has the same personality. They're both out for themselves, and if they don't get their way, they become hostile."

She goes on to say that when she's around Leanne, she can't help but remember her painful divorce from her husband. "I tried to make things amiable for the girls' sake, but that was naïve on my part. I should have known that my husband would not be cooperative; he's the kind who plays hardball financially and emotionally, and I staggered out of that marriage a lot poorer, disillusioned, and disgusted by how cruel he'd been."

Gloria says she feels guilty about letting her feelings about her ex-husband affect her relations with Leanne. "I know that's unfair. She's not him, and I try to keep the two of them separate in my mind. For a while, when I visited her in Los Angeles, I thought I was succeeding, but since then, I have had a hard time seeing her as herself, not just him, because she's so much like him."

We have heard stories about daughters who resemble an alcoholic father, a browbeating older sister, or another hurtful person in the mother's life—but most often, mothers talk about daughters who are like their own problematic mothers.

One woman was bruised by her mother's rejection growing up, and as a result, she did everything possible to give her daughter an abundance of love, support, and encouragement. But despite her efforts, her adult daughter has turned out to have a dismissive, uncaring attitude toward her that mirrors that of her own mother. It is there in her voice, her frown, and in the way she determinedly turns her back. Having a daughter like this is very painful and reawakens the vulnerability she suffered in the past. She says she repeats a mantra to herself when she is around her: "My daughter is not my mother. My daughter is not my mother." Sometimes it works. Often it doesn't.

When situations like these exist, the unresolved feelings from the past intrude. Anger, hurt, frustration, and feelings of rejection still reside within the mother, making it hard for her to find a loving bridge to connect to her daughter.

Margo tells us that she grew up as the middle child in a contentious working-class family. Her parents quarreled nightly, money was an ongoing issue, and there was worry about her younger brother who was unsuccessful in school. "My mom became seriously depressed when I was about twelve," she says. "Before that, I remember her taking care of our family, scolding me if I made a mess or went outside without enough warm clothes. I wasn't close to her, but she was there watching over me, a predictable part of my life. But then she took to her bed, closed the bedroom door, and days would go by when I didn't see her. It was a sad, lonely time. Since I was the only other female in our family, all the work fell on me. My older brother was exempt because he was the family star, the younger one was seen as the baby, and my dad always worked overtime. My *bubbe* tried to help—she came to see us several times a day—but her arthritis was bad by that time, and she had too much to do taking care of her own apartment and my grandfather. I'd rush home from school, tidy the house, and cook dinner for all of them, and then I'd clean up and try to get my homework done. I was furious, and most of all I was upset at my mom for abandoning me like that. I really needed her—I was just beginning to menstruate and my hormones were raging—and it seemed like she'd gone on strike."

Margo's eyes mist as she remembers that painful time. "I can understand her better now—she was overwhelmed by the stress in our family and suffering from depression—but I never completely forgave her. There's still a part of me that asks why she let that happen, even though I know she couldn't help being ill. She got better bit by bit, but the damage had already been done."

"And now you have a depressed daughter," we say.

Margo lifts an eyebrow. "Tell me about it."

"That must be really hard."

"It pushes every one of my buttons. If Elise had to have something wrong with her, I wish it were something that didn't remind me of my mother. It drives me crazy to have her holed up in that cottage, not doing anything. I remember standing outside the door to my mother's room, wanting so much to knock, wanting to get her out of there, but I'd finally walk away, completely intimidated by that closed door. Now I find myself outside the cottage, feeling that same way. Should I knock on the door and disturb my daughter? Should I do something to get her up and going? I'm damned if I do, damned if I don't. Just like when my mother was depressed." Margo stops. "That's an exaggeration, I know. My mother and my daughter are two very different people, and their situations aren't the same. It's just that emotionally I boomerang back to being a twelve-year-old child, dealing with this."

Margo's situation is very painful to navigate, but she continues to try to find a way to make authentic and loving contact with her daughter. She tells us, however, about a childhood friend who has made the decision to avoid her daughter because of a disturbing, unresolved echo from the past.

"The woman's mother was an alcoholic during her childhood, and when she was drunk she'd unleash a stream of invective at my friend, screaming that she was a stupid, ugly child," Margo says. "I saw it happening myself when I went to her house to play, and it was horrible to witness. My friend was seared by her rage and couldn't understand why she was being treated so cruelly. As an adult she realized the abuse was the liquor talking, but that didn't alleviate her childhood pain. Now her daughter drinks too much and becomes verbally abusive when she is drunk. It's such a tragedy. The mother says she can't handle it, and she doesn't want anything to do with her daughter. She avoids her at family gatherings and other places, making herself as small as she can if she has to be around her. It's all she can manage."

"That's so sad," we say.

"Especially because my friend doesn't have any other children. When things are hard with Elise, I still have my son."

The Importance of Values

Mothers identify temperament as very important in determining how close they are to their daughters, but they tell us that values also play a significant role. When their values—all those ethical and moral principles or standards of behavior that shape their lives—are embraced by their daughters, they have a deep sense of satisfaction. Even if their different temperaments make intimacy difficult, they know that they and their daughters share the same vision of the best way to live, and this goes a long distance toward smoothing out the rough edges between them.

Florence, the sixth and final mother we include here, has always been guided by her deeply held values. As a professor of public health at a local university, she has devoted her professional life to community service, and she continues now, at seventy-two, to consult on research about the spread of hepatitis C among young black males. She sits on several nonprofit boards and is respected as a person of wide experience and accomplishment. Through the years she also has been deeply committed to her extended family, a network of some forty people that includes Harriet, her oldest daughter, one son, and a much younger daughter, Rhonda. Eighteen months ago, James, her husband of forty-five years, died, but she continues to be central to all of her family, offering advice and direction.

With her silver hair, dark skin, and distinguished bearing, Florence is the picture of a successful professional woman. She's usually serious but breaks into a wide smile when she describes what it was like in their household when the children were young. "Oh, my, what a circus. This one running here, that one running there, and James and I back and forth to work. But we managed to bring up those kids, plus my sister's two boys who lived with us for a while, and we tried to instill good values in all of them. We taught them about the importance of community service, accomplishment, and family solidarity, and we did our best to set them on the right path."

Florence feels that Harriet, her oldest child, especially absorbed her values. "She's the head of a successful national arts organization, based in Washington, DC, and works tirelessly to bring attention to the talent and creativity of young black people from under-resourced backgrounds. She's completely devoted to this project and has received many honors for her accomplishments. Our areas of expertise are different, but we both feel the same way about helping our people get ahead."

"What about commitment to the family?" we ask.

"Harriet's like me in that way, too. She can't be as involved as I am because she lives so far away, but she keeps up as best she can, staying in touch with all of them, remembering their birthdays. My cousin's girl lives with her now because she was having trouble with drugs and needed straightening out, and other family members have come and gone over the years. We all know she is there to help in a crisis because she's that kind of person."

Florence is proud of Harriet and pleased that she mirrors her values. She says it makes it easy to be with her because they care about the same things. "She calls me every few days to see how I'm doing. We always end up talking about an event she's organizing or an issue that has arisen at work, and she asks about the research I'm doing. Sometimes it's like we're two colleagues having a conversation, and that's very satisfying."

Pat is another mother who appreciates that she and her daughter share the same values. "We don't look much alike—I'm a lot heavier, for one thing—but we have so much in common. I've been a hard worker all my life, and so has she. We value that, and we believe in fairness—treating people with respect and not taking advantage of them. I see her up close in her pet grooming business, and I know that's how she operates." Pat tells us that this sense of shared values has been apparent since Terri graduated from high school. "It goes a long distance towards bringing us together," she says. "I can count on her to behave properly because she lives by her values, and I do, too."

Sometimes the similarity between mothers' and daughters' values isn't as obvious as it is with Florence and Pat. One woman, a highly respected author, told us that she cares most about telling the truth as she knows it. She is respected for creating a sense of intimacy and candor in her memoir and nonfiction books, revealing painful events and feelings in a familiar way. She lives conventionally in a country farmhouse with a devoted husband and their dogs, cats, and chickens, but her daughter has always been a flamboyant rule-bender. Now fifty, she says that no gender fits who she truly is, and she is trying out a variety of new identities in a public way. At first the mother was shocked, but she has come to realize that her daughter's exploration of her gender identity is akin to her own search for truth in her writing.

The two women have always had a close bond, despite their apparent differences, and the mother now understands that it is due, at least in part, to the fact that they share the same values. Their styles might be very different, but they are not as far apart as they first appear. As she says with a certain amount of pride, "It turns out that the fruit did not fall very far from this tree."

When Values Are Different

Shared values seem to be a glue, and mothers say they really appreciate them when they exist. But we know many women who struggle to relate to daughters with priorities that are antithetical to their own. These differences often cause them to doubt themselves because they feel they did not "do it right" as mothers or somehow failed them.

We interviewed a woman who is deeply embedded in family and community, contributing her time and resources to those in need. She's known in her circles for her generosity and being the first one to step up in a crisis. Her daughter is a survivalist, eating off the land and hauling water from a nearby spring, and she lives alone, relating to people as little as possible. Although the mother admires her daughter's fortitude, she can't understand why she has chosen to lead such an isolated life. Her daughter's highest priority seems to be living independently, while hers is taking care of others. She feels that she failed in raising her because she was unable to transmit her moral and ethical values. But then again, she wonders if her daughter made these choices because she was too engaged with others when she was growing up and inadvertently ignored her needs. She says that when she is reminded of the differences between them in the way they live, she feels like she gave birth to a stranger.

We have spoken with first- and second-generation immigrant mothers whose daughters are moving comfortably through worlds they had never imagined—technology startups, officers in banks and businesses, administrators of educational institutions. These women talk about a sense of personal gratification that their daughters are able to make their dreams materialize. But at the same time, they worry that their values of home and cultural continuity have dissolved. They fear being left behind, unable to understand or engage much of these new worlds their daughters so easily inhabit.

A woman who emigrated as a teenager to the United States from China tells us that she is confused by her daughter and fears she is losing her. The daughter has an important administrative job in an international corporation, but unlike her brothers and sisters, she hardly is involved with the family. Recently her uncle had heart surgery, and she only called once to see how he was doing. The mother tried to talk to her about her absence, saying she should care more about him and the rest of them, but the daughter firmly responded by telling her that she has other commitments and a different way of life, and shouldn't be expected to follow in the same tradition as she does. The mother says she didn't know how to answer her.

Florence describes her confusion about the values of her younger daughter, Rhonda. "I don't understand what happened to her. The things that mean something to me—service, accomplishment, family—don't seem to mean much to her. She's bright, but she never finished college and doesn't seem to care about education or getting ahead. She has talent as a writer and is working on a novel, or at least that's what she says, but I doubt it will go anywhere. She doesn't try hard enough at anything. Men come and go, but no one sticks. It's like she and I are two separate species. I am respectful in my behavior, of course, but her choices confound me."

Florence grew up in Chicago with parents who sacrificed

so that their five children could move ahead in life. They've all had long, distinguished careers, a triumph for the family. But Rhonda seems to embody ways of being that are antithetical to the family tradition, and this is unsettling for Florence.

We interviewed a woman who is also puzzled by her daughter's choices. She's determined to support and stand by her but is bewildered by her far more conservative set of values. Her daughter and husband homeschool their children and control all the cultural stimuli that come into their lives, and the mother is especially concerned about how this will affect her grandchildren's future.

She says that the hardest part is that she has to step back, let go, and honor that her daughter is on her own path and needs to work out her way of parenting. What is most troubling is that her daughter and husband subscribe to values of purity and individualism and have a very rigid idea about what is and is not okay. Only carefully selected books, ideas, and technology are allowed in the home and in the children's lives. There is not, in the mother's mind, a normal, healthy flow of people and a wide, stimulating range of conversation. As grandparents, she and her husband are instructed very carefully about which gifts they can bring, what activities they can suggest, even what they can say. She feels that she's not getting the best of these grandkids, and they certainly are not getting the best of her. For a woman who has always emphasized openness and learning from others, this is a great loss and very difficult to accept.

We have heard a similar story about the effects of different values from a woman with a long history of feminist activism. Her daughter's husband is an outspoken right-wing advocate, and considers himself to be the undisputed head of the family. As such, he makes all the major decisions for her daughter and their children. Dissent is seldom allowed, and the mother tells us how despondent she feels about her daughter's choice to live in this kind of marriage, which is for her a repudiation of everything she has spent her life championing.

She says that she has stretched her heart muscle to the extent she never believed possible to continue loving her daughter. When she goes to visit, she can hardly bear to see the distance between them. Yet even with the ache of having to bridge this gulf, she fiercely insists on her attachment to her daughter. She says she has never fought for love so passionately and so relentlessly. This situation has taught her what love is: her heart is continually broken, but she has learned that one can go forward with a broken heart. As she says, mothers do it all the time.

Mothers Accommodate to Their Daughters' Values

With few exceptions, we have found that mothers do their best to accommodate to the values their daughters embrace, even if they are unfamiliar and alienating. This is because it's more important to them to maintain their relationships with their daughters than to create rifts that might exclude them from their lives or the developing lives of their grandchildren.

One mother told us that her daughter grew up in their local synagogue but converted to paganism as an adult and is now part of a coven in Minnesota. She is struggling financially, at least in part because of her contributions to her coven, but the mother is sending her money each month because she wants to be sure her grandchildren have all the resources they may need. While she disagrees with many things in her daughter's life and is very disappointed that she rejected Judaism, she doesn't want to risk losing contact with her and her grandchildren by behaving in a way that might cause a separation between them. She says she has always been clear within herself that she didn't raise her daughter to be the same as she is but to follow her own path, whatever that might be; her daughter is a grown woman and gets to live as she chooses. That's the best she can do. Actually that's all she can do.

Mothers work hard to hold and maintain their relationships with their daughters in ways that leave room for their different values. This sometimes means they must shift, alter, heighten, or diminish certain aspects of themselves.

Florence reflected on the contradictory feelings she has toward Rhonda. "When she comes to visit, I'm glad to see her. Her smile wins my heart, and it always has. I couldn't ask for a more loving, charming daughter, at least when she's around. But the fact that she doesn't have meaningful work weighs on me because I believe that everyone should contribute to society as best they can. If I bring up this subject, we argue about it. She says she doesn't want to live as I do, striving to succeed and not taking time for pleasure. She values free, creative expression most of all, and that's why she's chosen to write this novel. I disagree with what matters most to her, but I keep my thoughts to myself. I don't have to keep trying to convince her."

After a long silence, Florence took a deep breath and continued, "It's all so complicated. Despite my feelings about Rhonda's way of life, I'd say we're close to each other. That goes a long way in our family."

Most mothers seem to appreciate it when they and their daughters share at least some of the same worldview. It makes it easier to understand one another. However, we know a few mothers who feel that having different values is a positive thing, and they prefer that to having too much similarity.

One woman we interviewed provides a powerful example of this preference for difference. When her daughter was in her early twenties, the mother had a lover who needed a lot of emotional attention and care. Her daughter started a relationship with someone who was painfully similar to this man, and the mother feared that her choice was the result of the difficulty she seemed to be having growing up and leading her own life. She was disturbed by the obvious parallels, and when the relationship ended and her daughter began to realize her own distinct preferences in both partners and work, she was relieved.

Now, decades later, her daughter has well-defined values that are her own, and this allows for a kind of space and difference that makes for a rich and unique form of connection between them. She is temperamentally much like her mother, and they are able to read one another almost too easily and can get into emotional tangles that way. This mother has concluded that she and her daughter have a freer, less complicated intimacy when they relate through their otherness.

When There Is More Than One Daughter

No two mother-daughter relationships are alike. We had a long interview with a woman who is keenly aware of the subtleties that exist between herself and her two daughters. Temperamentally the oldest one has always been timid and watchful while her younger sister couldn't wait to race into new experiences, make new friends, and explore unfamiliar places. She's like her mother in that way. Both daughters are middle-aged now, and temperamentally, at least, little has changed. The younger daughter is ready to join the mother on any adventure while the older one holds back, anticipates problems, and is hesitant to consider something unexpected.

There is a reversal, however, when it comes to values. The older, timid daughter and her mother are both committed to working for racial and economic justice, and the daughter teaches sociology at a city college while the mother is an activist and organizer. The two of them talk for hours about the politics of what is needed to create successful and lasting structural change. Her younger daughter, in comparison, values spontaneity and creativity most of all, and her work as a printmaker reflects these choices.

This mom says that even though she and her younger daughter are more alike temperamentally, she and her older child have more values in common. When the three of them get together, as they do a few times a year, the mother is careful that they don't veer too much in one direction or another so that everyone will be included in the conversation.

We've spoken with a few women who have three or more

daughters, which makes for an even more complicated mix of temperaments and values. One freewheeling, expressive mother tells us that her good-natured oldest daughter responds openly when she asks her what she's thinking and feeling. But the second, who has a more contained personality, withdraws and becomes silent. The third daughter gets mad at her for being too intrusive. Even in this one small area of interacting, the mother has to keep these widely varying responses in mind and act appropriately. Her tendency is to push them all to talk openly because she values honest exchange, but that works with only one of them.

Shouldn't We Be Similar?

Given a choice, most mothers say they'd rather that their daughters be more like them than different. They tell us that even at this time in their lives, when they are growing old and their daughters have long ago left their homes, they still carry a desire to share a certain "sameness" with them, although in so many cases it is clear that won't happen to the degree they wish.

The question is why mothers yearn for daughters to be like them. It seems to us that this does not occur as often with sons—although we can't say for certain since we did not interview women in depth about these relationships. Still, we have heard from many that the expectation of "otherness" is at the root of their relationships with their sons rather than "sameness." They are of different genders, after all.

Perhaps now, when gender is being explored and lived in

new ways, the same assumptions aren't being made, but for women who came to motherhood in the mid-twentieth century, gender was a fixed matter. As Florence reports, "My son, my middle child, stops by to help me with things like the broken dishwasher or a tree that has fallen. But he has a wife and three kids and a business he's just started, so there's only so much time. I understand that. He's a man, with a man's responsibilities."

Margo also doesn't expect as much from her son as she does from her daughter. "My son is a joy, and he always has been. I'd say he and I are more alike in our personalities, but I'm a woman and he's a gay man, and there's that separation between us. It's just a fact."

Mothers and daughters, however, have similar bodies and go through the same physical stages over the course of the years: the budding breasts, the rush of hormones, the monthly cycles, the shifts in body fat and muscle, menopause and aging. Many of them share the experience of childbirth. Because of their similar bodies, the notion of "sameness" is at the root of their relationship, heightened by the assumptions society makes about them as women. They are socialized to be more emotionally nurturing and supportive than the men around them, expected to be caretakers, and occupy similar societal roles.

There is a mystique about women in families being alike: generation to generation, the story goes. Women being women together. The men come and go, but the strength of the family resides with the women.

Margo shows us a corner table in her library where she displays the photographs of the women in her family, carefully lined up in their silver frames. "I come here often, looking at them," she says to us. "I'm sentimental, I admit it, but they give me strength. There they all are—my great-grandmother in this sepia photo, and my grandmother and her three sisters before they immigrated. And my mom all dressed up on the day she married, and her holding me when I was a baby, and me again when I graduated from college. Then me, a new mom, with baby Elise, and Elise playing in the yard when she was seven, running through the leaves. All of us, a chain of women."

A chain through the generations. No wonder, then, that women want their daughters to be familiar, or at least knowable. The dream is that the boundaries between them—already so permeable because of their similar bodies and societal roles—will be erased so that they are one in this long line of tradition.

CHAPTER THREE

Under the Surface

Many mothers who raised daughters in the 1960s and 1970s were determined that they grow up to be free and independent adult women. They vowed to accept and love them for who they were, rather than insist on them meeting their expectations or demands. The enormous cultural changes taking place at this time were consistent with their way of thinking about motherhood and further strengthened their resolve.

The shackles from their own upbringing would be broken by this kinder, more supportive style of mothering—or at least that was their vision. But mother-daughter relationships didn't always turn out as they wanted. Some were troubled from the beginning, others faltered along the way, and painful divorces, messy family dynamics, traumatic events, and incidents of abuse kept this vision from materializing.

The past continues to exist in the present. Mothers sense it affecting their daughters, even if it isn't named or mentioned. Misunderstandings or struggles emerge that have more to do with what happened decades ago, surprising them with the power of old feelings to create havoc.

Determined to Be Different

Every mother has a story to tell about her relationship with her daughter and its history. Typically these stories start far back in the mothers' lives, when they themselves were young. How they were mothered and what happened to them as daughters influenced what kind of mothers they wanted to be. Their early experiences, along with the emergence of new cultural norms, set the stage for the vision of mothering they embraced.

Cindy, like many women of her generation, felt strongly that she did not want to be like her own mother. "When I was little, we lived in a Baltimore suburb, and my mom was a proper, refined lady. Everything was done by the rulebook. I had to eat a certain way, dress a certain way, act a certain way, and if I didn't, I was spanked or locked in my room. This was practically a daily occurrence. My older brother was quiet and obedient, the good child, the one who made my mother proud, but I was always a great disappointment. I was too scrawny, too messy; I made too much noise and was naughty at school. The only thing I did well was draw and paint, but that didn't impress her."

Cindy's mother, like so many women who raised daughters in the 1940s and 1950s, was shaped by the experience of the Great Depression and World War II. She believed in the values of self-sacrifice and hard work, doling out discipline more often than praise and hugs. Middle-class women of her generation were expected to center their lives on their families and hold jobs only if financially necessary.

Cindy looks out the window of her art studio as she continues to describe growing up with her mother. "I suppose she wasn't very happy. My dad traveled for work and stayed away for days at a time, so she was stuck alone in that house with just us two kids and our pet dog and turtles. She must have been so bored. But she didn't reveal her feelings about anything, so I had no idea what she felt. I mostly knew her as a cranky, hard-to-please person who told me what to do—and as a mother who didn't love me."

Many women speak about the emotional inaccessibility of their own mothers during those decades. They describe them as adults who, in retrospect, raised them the best way they were able but did not talk about their own struggles, hopes, or dreams. Instead they mothered. Their reticence to reveal themselves to their daughters was identified as a deep and continuing loss by the women we interviewed.

Cindy tells us, "There must have been so much more to her than that duty-bound, irritable surface. But I rebelled early on, deciding I'd never be anything like her. I'd be an artist, a free and expressive person, and nobody would ever hold me back. I ran off to New York after high school, supported myself with odd jobs, and hung out in Greenwich Village. When I got pregnant at nineteen, I wanted to have the baby and figured my boyfriend and I would just carry it around with us as we led our crazy life creating art, getting high, and living with friends in one place or another." Cindy stops for a moment. "Talk about being irresponsible."

Cindy's boyfriend was more realistic than she about the demands ahead, however, and insisted they marry before Frida was born. A friend lent them a tiny fifth floor apartment, and they settled into this next chapter of their lives.

"What kind of mother did you want to be?" we ask.

"I was going to reverse my childhood," Cindy says. "I wanted to give Frida lots of love and room to explore on her own. No rules, no demands, no discipline. She'd have a strong sense of confidence because she'd be raised to be independent. I was determined to tell her what I was thinking and feeling, and she'd know me in a way I never knew my own mother."

Cindy's story is not at all unusual. The desire in those years was to throw out the old and bring in the new, and young mothers inhabited a landscape that was in a state of enormous upheaval. The cultural patterns of the past two decades had morphed into a kaleidoscope of new possibilities. Battles raged over American's involvement in Vietnam, a growing civil rights movement was challenging the racial status quo, and the growth of the second wave of feminism with all the unexamined assumptions of gender upended the America of the 1940s and 1950s.

Women began to step into an expanded self beyond the confines of tradition. This was the beginning of second-wave feminism, a time of determined rejection of old roles and the bumpy creation of new ones. A different language was taking shape, a vocabulary of intimacy that was based on openness and sharing. In this emerging world, the highest values were physical affection, verbal communication, freedom, and pride in experimentation. Mothers felt certain that their daughters would flourish with kind words and minimal guidance.

Like Mother, Like Daughter

Cindy's eyes have a faraway look as she talks about her dreams for raising Frida, but she pauses when we ask her how it turned out.

"Well. . ." She draws out the word. "Everything was more complicated than I thought it would be."

Cindy and her young husband lived on the margin, scrambling to support themselves and their art projects, and now, a child. "At first, when Frida was little, I was totally wrapped up in her, but then my husband and I started to have problems. He was able to sell some of his paintings, so it made sense that he be free to paint every day and I be the one to take care of her. At nights I waited tables at an Italian restaurant to earn more money, but that meant I had no time for my own creative work, and I was wildly jealous of his freedom and success. He wanted an open marriage; I went along with him, although that was never anything I would have wanted, and we argued about that and everything else. Frida, who was about three, was turning into a little martinet. I remember one day I served her lunch on her plastic ducky plate, but the food was jumbled together rather than separated into little piles as she liked, and she howled and threw everything on the floor. I was so angry that I reached over and slapped her, which made her howl all the more, and then I ran into the bathroom and threw up. I felt like I'd turned into my mother. I vowed I'd never raise my hand to her again."

In the following years, Cindy tried as hard as she could to be a good mother. Through the breakup and divorce from her husband, through the lovers that followed and a second marriage that collapsed, through the many moves and the struggle to survive, she held in mind this desire to help Frida be independent and confident. "How well did your efforts succeed?" we ask her.

"Honestly, it's mixed," she answers. "I gave her some things I didn't have, like freedom and independence, and I never hit her again, but in many ways I ignored some of her greatest needs. It took me a long time to realize, but I neglected her even though my heart was in the right place."

Benign Neglect

As women look back on their mothering during the tumultuous decades of the mid-twentieth century, many say it can best be summarized as benign neglect. At the time they were convinced they were doing the right thing by giving their daughters the freedom they'd never had, but their certainty has diminished through the years. Now they are left with at least the beginnings of an understanding that they did not provide enough structure or stability and missed out on taking care of their essential needs.

Cindy says, "I always gave Frida a lot of love, but I should have known she was being hurt by how we lived. I was too lax and preoccupied. I left her with people she shouldn't have been around and kept her out much too late at night because there was no money for babysitters. No wonder she still judges me for being irresponsible."

When we began our interviews, we had no idea that so many mothers would tell us that their current relationships with their daughters are deeply affected by how carelessly they mothered or how uninvolved they were with their daughters' experience. It makes sense: daughters still carry wounds from living in unsupervised situations, or being exposed at a too-young age to adult use of alcohol and drugs, or yanked from one home or school to another.

Mothers say they feel both responsible and defensive. Some are able to face what happened during those early child-raising years, but others find the memories still too raw. The past has been pushed back as they have moved on—but it hasn't disappeared. Mothers still notice their daughters reacting to something they say or do as though the past were fully present, and they find themselves tensing up with guilt or shame about how they inadvertently caused wounds, even though they loved their daughters and were only trying to create a world that would allow them a greater sense of freedom.

A Silent Rebuke

Many of the women we interview are grandmothers now. They are baffled by the ways that child-rearing has become so much more structured with its play dates and after-school lessons, and remember how they used to send their daughters out to play without knowing where they were going, only with the instructions to be home in time for dinner. They scoff at helicopter parenting and think their grandchildren need less structure and more freedom. The changes that have taken place in child-rearing unsettle them because they seem to be a silent rebuke from their daughters, a way of pointing the finger at the lack of consistency, order, and safety they provided for them when they were young and vulnerable.

Cindy describes Frida's family. "She lives with her husband and two girls in Marin County, across the bridge from San Francisco. They're always busy, and when I go there, nobody has time to sit for a visit. You wouldn't believe the schedule they keep, never a free moment, always rushing here and there for lessons or sports, and there's so much pressure on the kids. Where is the fun in living like that, the satisfaction?"

Cindy says it's sad that parents feel they have to micromanage their children so much these days. "There is so much fear and anxiety in the world. But the pendulum has swung too far from the pole of uninvolved parenting to the pole of too much control and supervision."

We ask her what she thinks mothering is like for Frida. "She tries so hard to be the perfect mother and control things that can't be controlled. She's running herself into the ground. I've hinted at this a few times, but she always tells me she doesn't want her kids to experience the lack of structure she had in her childhood." She pauses. "Well, it's her choice."

Divorce and its Unintended Consequences

Most mothers tell us that their dream of raising their daughters in new, improved ways ran into difficulty, sometimes early on. They wanted to be ever-loving, ever-accepting, and ever-encouraging but ended up hurting their daughters by not providing enough structure or consistency.

The damage went beyond that, however. As they look back, they regret that they didn't shield them better from the tensions that broke apart so many families. Many marriages crumbled during the 1960s, 1970s, and 1980s, when the mothers we interviewed were raising their girls. The divorce rate, which had been low during the 1950s, the "golden age of marriage," rose sharply so that by 1980 nearly one in two marriages didn't last. In that time of social experimentation and political ferment, women were elbowing their way forward into what they imagined would be fuller, more satisfying lives, and marriages that weren't solid enough to withstand the pressures of such a changing landscape were discarded. Many of the mothers we interviewed were part of this cadre of women who got divorced, and they recognize how deeply this affected and still affects their daughters.

The six women we focus on in this book are no strangers to divorce: Pat, Dolores, and Gloria each experienced one, and Cindy two. Florence's marriage to James, the father of her children, lasted forty-five years, but she had a disastrous short marriage and divorce before she met him. Margo has never been divorced, but listening to the difficulties of her clients, friends, and other family members allows her an intimate understanding.

Mothers who have been divorced tell us how very hard the experience was on their daughters. "It really tore Terri up," Pat acknowledges. "She thought we were a happy little family, and it came as a huge shock. I fought against the divorce, and there was a lot of screaming and tears, but my husband insisted. It turned out he'd been having an affair for over a year and wanted to marry the woman. Terri was twelve, and she went from being an outgoing, cheerful child to shutting herself up in her room, sullen and impossible to reach. She was like that most of her teen years and still says it was the worst time of her life."

"Does the divorce affect your relationship now?" we ask.

Pat looks away, taking time to find the right words. "I'd say Terri feels more responsible for me because of it. When my husband left, I was a basket case, and she felt she had to take care of me even though she was just a kid. She resented being in that position. I tried to be independent and not lean on her too much, but sometimes I couldn't help myself. It's almost forty years later now, but that same dynamic is there between us. I'm uneasy about asking her for things because I'm afraid she might become resentful, like she did after the divorce. She's a terrific daughter and we're so close these days, but I still worry that I'm too much for her. Sometimes she makes little remarks that make me wonder—like recently she asked me why I'm not spending more time with my friends. Maybe it was an innocent question, but it might have come from her feeling that I'm too dependent on her. I don't know."

"Did you check it out with her?" we ask.

"I thought about it," Pat replies, "but I didn't."

"Because?"

"She'd get irritated. She doesn't like being questioned about things she says."

Pat believes that if there had been no divorce, the underlying strain between them would not exist. "She wouldn't have to feel responsible for me, because my husband would be there. I tell her not to worry, but I can see that she does."

We've heard many stories about the effects of divorce on daughters. Terri was traumatized by it, and so were Gloria's two daughters.

As Gloria tells us, "Kris was eight and Leanne was ten years old when my husband and I split. Leading up to our separation, we had drifted apart and stopped sleeping together, and I was exploring my attraction to women. When my husband found out, he exploded in front of the girls, shouting that he was going to take them away from me because I was an unfit mother and a sick, perverted person. It was such an ugly scene. He lunged toward me, fists raised, and the girls and I screamed bloody murder until he backed off. They'll never forget that moment. It left deep scars, even to this day."

Daughters of divorce not only experienced horrifying episodes like this one but they had to deal with their worlds falling apart. Gloria's household changed radically after the divorce. Leanne blamed her for the breakup and withdrew from her, and Kris loyally defended her, clinging to her for solace. In the years that followed, this split in allegiance increased. As Gloria remembers, "When Leanne was fourteen and announced that she wanted to move in full time with her dad, I was really hurt. By that time he had remarried, and his new wife fussed over her, buying her expensive new clothes and teaching her how to use makeup, things I never did. I'm pretty sure my ex-husband continued to trash me for being a lesbian and a bad mother all that time. Thankfully Kris resisted this and seemed happy to live with me, but I hated that there was this breach with Leanne."

The involvement of Gloria's ex-husband's in Leanne's life did not represent the norm in mid-twentieth-century America. Many fathers disappeared from active parenting, and they visited with their children on court-determined days and contributed money under duress for their upkeep. These arrangements left mothers trying to provide for themselves and their children on low wages, with limited help from the governmental safety net that existed then. This state of economic uncertainty left children vulnerable, and many became latchkey kids, waiting for their exhausted moms to get home from work, or they were passed from one babysitter to the next. Cindy was among those mothers who struggled to support herself and Frida. Although she had wanted the divorce—she'd had enough of fighting with her husband—she was ill-prepared to care for her six-year-old child. She stayed in Greenwich Village after the divorce, still dreaming of becoming an artist, but had no time to develop her creativity. Her ex-husband had moved to England, and her parents disapproved of the life she was leading and refused to help her financially. "I continued to waitress most evenings at the Italian restaurant and took a day job at an art store," she says. "But that meant I hardly saw Frida. I dropped her off at school in the morning, a babysitter picked her up afterwards, and then I'd rush home for dinner. In the evenings I usually brought her along with me to the restaurant. The owner was kind and let her stay in the back room, where she'd fall asleep, but I'd have to awaken her at the end of my shift to walk home late at night. It was a terrible time for her."

Yet, despite her grueling work schedule, Cindy felt pleased she had been freed from an unsatisfying marriage. When she wasn't working on the weekends, she shared ideas with other artists, attended art openings and book readings, and became involved in anti-Vietnam War activities, taking Frida along on marches. She and her friends experimented with drugs, and she began to take lovers.

"That period in my life was fantastic for me but not for Frida," she tells us. "Strange people were coming in and out of our apartment at all hours, and the older she got, the more she complained."

Blended Families

Cindy is a self-described free spirit, but even she felt the need for more stability. When Frida was ten, she met a man with a successful printing business on Long Island, and almost on a whim, decided to marry him, although that meant leaving Greenwich Village and her friends behind. In her mind she'd have the security she'd missed and the time to develop herself as an artist, and Frida would be in a better environment.

"What a mistake," Cindy tells us. "It turned out that my new husband and Frida absolutely did not get along. He'd never lived with a child before and wanted her to be silent and obedient, but she had a mind of her own. I'd raised her that way. She didn't like him or his house, and she hated her new school. My husband demanded all my attention and didn't want to be bothered with her, but there she was, taking up space. I was caught in the middle, trying to please both of them. It was an impossible situation, and I didn't handle it very well. I should have left with Frida right away, but instead I stayed for four years, trying to make it work."

"How did Frida feel about this?" we ask, already guessing the answer.

"She was furious. She said I didn't protect her enough." Cindy's voice drops and she stares out the window. "And she was right."

Many of the divorced mothers we interviewed have created new families through the years, some of which have endured and others which haven't. Daughters have found themselves in a variety of family constellations with a changing cast of characters: stepparents or mothers' new partners, half- or step-siblings, assorted old and new grandparents, aunts, and uncles, and a shifting group of family friends. They have witnessed the beginnings and often the endings of these attempts at family-making by their mothers.

Blended families appear to have worked best when the mother and daughter remained close, or when the new step-father or partner was especially respectful of the connection between them, or when everybody loved or at least liked each other. Daughters do not seem to have a lot of emotional residue from living in blended families such as these. But often, as with Cindy, the blended family didn't work out, and daughters still carry old feelings of resentment, abandonment, and loss.

Gloria also has a story to tell about this time in her life. "A year after my divorce, the woman I'd been dating and her teen-aged son moved in with us, and she and I tried to make a family. Leanne was resentful and nasty to her. Neither of my daughters liked her son, who teased them mercilessly, and my girlfriend had no control over him. Our relationship bottomed out with all this stress, and after two years we decided it was over. I've always thought that experience was part of why Leanne insisted on living with her dad."

"Do you think it still affects your relationship?" we ask.

"It broke some kind of trust between us. She saw me as the mother who chose someone else over her and turned her life upside down. Not only that, but I pressured her to go along with the arrangement, disregarding her feelings. She was angry at me then, and she still has that edge toward me now."

"And Kris?"

"She didn't like my girlfriend either, but she rolled with the situation."

"Why do you think that was?"

Gloria pauses for a moment. "It's her temperament. Kris has always been more easygoing and forgiving."

Family Dynamics

Every family has its own set of dynamics operating under the surface. The patterns that were established in the past often remain as the years go by and affect how mothers and daughters behave and feel about one another in the present. This happens both in families that were broken by divorce, like Gloria's, as well as those that remain intact, like Margo's.

Mothers spend hours telling us about the interactions and relationships of family members, the rivalries, attachments, angers, and hurts that have risen. We hear a great deal about who is close and who isn't and their understanding of why.

Gloria's story about Leanne's attachment to her father is not uncommon. Some mothers talk about their daughters being "Daddy's girls," even now that they are middle-aged, and say they are more likely to go to their fathers, not them, when they need help or comfort. The pairing of father and daughter, with the mother shunted to the sidelines, is perhaps the most common family dynamic mentioned.

As we have seen with Gloria, this attachment can be very disappointing for mothers. They entered motherhood assuming they'd be the preferred parent, and something seems off balance or wrong if that doesn't materialize. They worry about

what they did or didn't do and become discouraged if the attachment continues into their daughter's midlife, as it sometimes does. As Gloria says, "In my head I can accept that
Leanne cares more about her father than me, but it still hurts."

Yet other mothers are more accepting of this situation.
Florence took it in her stride when it became clear that Rhonda
preferred her father. "James was a sweet, good man, and she'd
curl up next to him, telling him all her troubles even when she
was little, and he'd listen patiently. With me, there was always
more distance. But I had enough other children around and a
lot of responsibilities, so even though I was aware of her attachment to him, it didn't bother me."

When we ask Florence why she thinks her husband and
daughter had such a strong connection, she shrugs. "Their personalities fit better. James was a giver, and Rhonda always
wanted and needed a lot of attention and love. If she fell down,
he'd run over and comfort her right away while I waited to see
if she'd get up by herself. I was a more demanding parent and
made my kids act properly and be respectful to others. She
didn't like that so much." Florence stops for a moment, and
sadness fills in her eyes. "And now James is gone." She shakes
her head. "I miss him. And I know Rhonda does, too. When
she comes to visit me, she sometimes looks at his photograph
and cries."

"Have things changed between you and Rhonda since your
husband passed?"

"No, and I don't think they will. Rhonda remained tied to
him until the end. She had something special for her daddy and
there will always be a hole where that was. I can't fill it up."

Florence tells us that everyone in the family knew that

Rhonda was her father's favored child. "That caused a lot of jealousy and hurt feelings. My two older kids got together and picked on her sometimes, and she'd go crying to her father. He'd tell them to stop, but it just made it worse."

Even now Florence's two older children are not very involved with Rhonda. "The separation between them widened as they grew up," she says, "and they don't have much to do with each other. My son lives fifteen minutes away from her, but I don't think either one lifts up the phone. And when Rhonda traveled to Washington, DC, recently, she didn't even stay with Harriet. The exception is when James died and they all came together, at least for that brief moment."

The more we talk, the more we learn that the lack of harmony among Florence's children is a source of anguish for her. She grew up in a family where the siblings have always remained close, and she sees this as the way it should be. "When I'm gone, who will bring my children together?" she asks. "I worry about that a lot. People need family. But I've made the mistake of trying to change the way it is with them. I spoke to Harriet about trying to help Rhonda, and I talked to my son about inviting her over to his house, and then I talked to Rhonda about reaching out to the other two. But I hit a wall. I can't make them do these things. I've come to understand that I need to step away and let it be. Otherwise I get all torn up inside."

Florence tells us that the greatest source of antagonism is between her two daughters. Harriet judges Rhonda as irresponsible, and Rhonda is exasperated by her older sister's condescension. "I make sure to visit them separately, and I don't allow talk by one sister about the other," Florence says. "It's too easy for me to get in the middle, and then they both turn on me." She recounts a time after James's funeral when Rhonda came to her, upset about something Harriet had said. "It wasn't significant, just a little comment she probably took the wrong way. But I made the mistake of asking Harriet to apologize to her since Rhonda was in such a bad state. This set Harriet off. 'She isn't the only one around here who lost a father,' she muttered. I let that remark go, but she was resentful. And then Rhonda was hurt because her sister never apologized. It's a no-win situation, and I try not to have anything to do with it. But it affects my relationship with both of them."

Antagonism in families comes in many shapes and forms. We hear about daughters who prefer their fathers to their mothers, and daughters who don't get along with each other, making their mothers miserable. Another painful triangle exists when mothers are pulled between their daughters and their husbands or partners.

Margo, for one, has been experiencing this for most of her daughter's life. "Don't get me wrong, Ted and I are great together," she says. "He's the love of my life. But even when Elise was little, he seemed to resent her existence. I always thought that was because she was the first child, and he didn't like that he got less of me after she was born. I know he loves her, but he's critical and says things that hurt her feelings. The bottom line is that he'd rather be alone with me, and he makes that very clear. Now that he's retired and has more time on his hands, he's getting even more this way."

"But there Elise is, living so close to you," we note.

"That bugs the hell out of Ted," Margo says. "God knows, I also wish Elise was independent and out on her own, and I'm unhappy about the situation. But when he starts talking about asking her to leave the cottage, I get defensive and angry. She's the only thing we fight about."

Margo tells us that Ted, who collects art as a sideline of his investment business, wants her to go away with him for two months to South America. "He says it's to locate some paintings for one of his wealthy clients, but I know it's to get away from the house so he'll have me all to himself. But frankly, I don't want to leave Elise and my grandson for that long. When I told him that, he exploded."

Margo and Ted have been fighting over her involvement with Elise for years. We've heard her side of the story, how split she is by her loyalty and love for both of them. If we were to ask Ted, he'd probably tell us how abandoned he has been by his wife, and Elise undoubtedly would say something about how rejected she is by both her parents. While everyone has their story, we're most interested in how this tension has affected Margo's experience as a mother. "In truth, I most often choose Ted over my daughter to keep the peace," she says. "I'm not proud of that. She must feel that I am letting let her down. There's a triangle in our family—Ted and me, and unfortunately Elise is the odd person out. I'm convinced this is one of the causes of her low self-esteem, and that makes me feel really guilty. I'm always trying to make up for it, even though I'm mad at her for not getting her life together."

Traumatic Events

Dolores, too, knows something about being in a painful triangle. She reminds us that Yolanda has always been closer to her mother and she feels like the loser in this configuration. "I accepted her preference when she was little, because my mom mostly took care of her while I was working all the time," Dolores says. "I hoped that would change when she was eleven and I brought her to Oakland, but unfortunately it didn't. She was unhappy about being separated from her grandmother and angry with me. Each year, when she went back to San Antonio for the summer, she fought returning in the fall, and each year I insisted she come. That didn't do us any good."

Mother and daughter lived together in Oakland in an uneasy truce, but their fights intensified when Yolanda entered high school. As Dolores says, "Our apartment was in a marginal neighborhood, and I worried about her. She looked older than her age, and I could see how vulnerable she was. I started to clamp down, setting rules, trying to protect her, and she hated that and rebelled against me."

Perhaps Dolores and Yolanda would have made it through the turbulent teenage years and reached some kind of understanding, but a disturbing event helped to shape a different outcome. "I discovered that she had a boyfriend, an older guy with his own car, and I forbade her from seeing him. One day I came home from work, went into her room, and saw that some of her things were missing, and I was sure she'd run off with her boyfriend. I got scared and called the police." That began a period of two weeks of waiting and worrying, with no word from Yolanda—until a call came from the police in El Paso. There had been an accident, a collision on the freeway, and the boyfriend had been seriously injured. Luckily Yolanda escaped with just some cuts and bruises. As Dolores says, "I flew to El Paso and stormed into the hospital. I was relieved she was okay, but I was really furious at her for running off like that. After leaving the hospital, we started to fight, and I said things I shouldn't have. She told me she hated me, and I said that I hated her, too. I yelled at her that she was no good, and she'd come to a bad end. Once those terrible words were out of my mouth, I could not take them back, even though they came from my anger and I didn't mean them at all."

Dolores tells us that they hardly spoke after they returned to Oakland. "Yolanda was worried about her boyfriend, but also, my words had done their damage. There was no compromise, no reconciliation. When she went to San Antonio soon after that for the summer, she had her *quinceañera*, and I flew down for it. But I stood on the sidelines and didn't feel welcome. And that was that. At the end of the summer Yolanda insisted that she stay in San Antonio, as she did each year, but this time I agreed to it. That's where she's been ever since."

Dolores's story of the trauma that led to the break in her relationship with Yolanda is especially sad, but not all traumatic events cause such disintegration. Some mothers say they became closer to their daughters because they shared the experience of a death in the family, or the need to deal with a disabled sibling or child, or a natural disaster that required everyone to pull together. The special bond that emerged from this intense life passage, they say, has remained through the years. They are the fortunate ones. Traumas, like Yolanda's car accident and Dolores's scalding words, much more often cause emotional distress and disconnection between mothers and daughters.

Legacy of Abuse

We've found that one of the most significant shapers of mother-daughter relationships is past physical and sexual abuse. A surprising number of mothers say that the long-term effects of earlier abuse are a cause of their current difficulties.

After telling us about Yolanda running away, Dolores reveals that she had an experience of abuse in her past. "When I look back at what I said to Yolanda that day in El Paso, I think there's a connection between that and something that happened to me when I was her age," she says. "My uncle, who was living with us in San Antonio at that time, molested me. At night he came into my room and reached under the blankets and into my pajama bottoms. I was scared and always pretended I was asleep and tried to hold very still. Once I tried to tell my mother what he was doing, but she loved her brother and got angry with me instead. She yelled that I was no good and I would come to a very bad end, the same words I used with Yolanda." Dolores drops her head, "It's a horrible thing, repeating such painful words from the mother to a daughter."

"Did you ever tell Yolanda what happened to you?" we ask.

She looks up at us. "When did I have the chance? Besides, it was a long time ago."

Mothers say that the abuse they experienced when they were young affected who they were as mothers and who they still are today. As Dolores tells us toward the end of our conversation, "My uncle's abuse and my mother's reaction made me who I am today. The experience left me feeling cynical and negative. Did that affect how I was as a mother to Yolanda? Of course it did."

Gloria, too, suffered from childhood abuse, beatings from her father. She discloses this piece of her history when she tells us that she never raised a hand to either of her daughters. "I can be proud about that," she says. "But that's because I had such a miserable experience being hit myself." She goes on to say that her beloved mother died when she was nine, leaving her alone with her father, an alcoholic who angrily whacked her with a switch cut from their almond tree. "Most of the time I didn't know why he was doing it or what I had done wrong. I had red stripes on my backside after he switched me, and I was ashamed of them and kept myself covered so nobody would see," she says. "Thankfully I had the memory of my mother's love, so I didn't view the world as all dangerous. But my father's violence frightened me and made me wary. I decided early on that I wasn't going to let anyone get too close to me."

"Did that affect how you were as a mother?"

"I'm sure it did. Honestly, I don't trust very many people even now. Judy, fortunately, is one of those I do. But when I'm around Leanne, I feel a well of distrust. It's an automatic response I have with people who seem to hold a lot of anger toward me, like she does."

Among the most painful conversations we have are with women whose daughters were sexually or physically abused. Often these mothers themselves experienced abuse as children and know firsthand the wounds it creates, making their guilt all the more agonizing.

Pat tells us of a time when Terri was fifteen. "After the divorce, she was suffering emotionally, and I tried everything I could to make things better for her. She wanted to learn to play the piano, so I arranged for her to take lessons from the man next door. Even though I sensed an eagerness on his part that seemed not quite right, I talked myself out of my instinct. Everything went okay for a while, and she really liked the lessons, but then one day he forced her onto the couch and groped her breasts. She wrenched away from him, and ran home screaming, terrified and confused. I felt terribly guilty that I hadn't better protected her, and I confronted him at once, but he denied everything. I told her to stay away from him and never go to his house again, but I've always felt ashamed that I didn't heed my original instinct that something was off with him, or at least lodge a formal complaint against him. What kind of lesson was that to teach her?"

Pat goes on to tell us how the abuse experience affected Terri. "She was already feeling closed off and resentful toward me because of the divorce, but I think that some of her trust for me died that day. My job as a mother was supposed to be to protect her, but I'd failed. I tried to make it better, telling her that I'd once had a similar kind of experience with my high school swimming coach, so I understood how horrible her experience was. But that was the wrong thing to say. If I knew how traumatic it was, why hadn't I protected her better?"

"How did you get from that experience to the closeness you have now?" we ask.

"It took a long time. After Terri graduated from high school, she went off on her own, living with friends, supporting herself with odd jobs, traveling when she could. I hardly saw her, which was really hard on me because I missed her so much. After about ten years, she moved back here and started to think about opening up her pet grooming business. She took a few business classes and asked for my help because of my bookkeeping experience. I was thrilled, and we started seeing each other more often until we ended up closer than I ever imagined."

"Have you spoken to her about the abuse in recent years?"

"It's better left alone," Pat says firmly. "There's no need to bring that subject up. I like to stay with what's positive and try to forget the negative."

From the Past to the Present

Mothers appreciate being able to talk about the past and how it has shaped their connections with their daughters. There is so much to say. Relationships are pliable and have been influenced by multiple internal and external forces over the years. Similarities and differences have played a role in how attuned mothers and daughters are, and the family dynamics under the surface have had their impact as well.

Yet mothers and daughters live in the present, and their relationships are what they are, for good or for bad. Perhaps in the future there will be an unexpected reconciliation or moments of greater closeness, but the connection will likely remain more or less as it already is. Too much history has gone by; too many patterns are set. What's missing is noted and sometimes mourned, and what's there is acknowledged and sometimes appreciated.

As mothers become older and closer to the end of their lives, they reflect more about these relationships and experience them in a heightened way. They question what has gone on in the past, wondering what it means, and understand in new ways that nobody's personality is going to change, the extrovert won't become the introvert, and the abused daughter isn't going to forget her trauma. For some, it's a time of discouragement and frustration, for others it's an opening to acceptance.

In the midst of this, life goes on. The past is just under the surface with all that is unsaid or intuited, but the present is much more important. It is where women continue to mother their midlife daughters in a variety of ways, where issues rise up and make themselves known, where love exists in all its complexity, and where they move slowly together toward the future and mothers' diminishment.

CHAPTER FOUR

Mothering in the Present Tense

Mothers remember when their young daughters were dependent on them for their protection and care, and they cooked for them, bathed them, and brushed their hair before bed. In those days they were clear about what was needed and the responsibilities they were expected to fulfill. Now that their daughters are in their forties or fifties, however, they often are confused about their roles and uncertain what mothering means at this time in their lives.

It's disorienting to think of themselves as actively mothering, they say. The shared history, the easy places, and the difficulties continue to exist in the relationship, but their daughters are fully grown, established in their own routines, and no longer needing them in the ways they once did. They are still mothers—that is not questioned—but even if they are very involved in their daughters' lives, they don't necessarily consider the things they do for them as mothering activities.

This lack of recognition seems to arise from the feeling that they and their daughters have grown to be equals over time. Although they're related and have a unique history, they're both adults and share many of the same experiences as women. They're not exactly friends, but there is more reciprocity between them than there was in the past. It would seem strange to many mothers to label what they do in this reconfigured relationship as *mothering*.

Some say they don't notice their mothering because it has become so routine. They give words of encouragement and offers of assistance without thought, and much of what they do for their daughters appears to come from habitual patterns rather than actions grounded in conscious intention. Only when they begin to think about their mothering and the energy that goes into it do they notice how hard they are trying, and they realize that they are still very much invested in this role.

Mothers also live in a culture where it is assumed that they have finished active mothering by the time their offspring have reached their middle years and are established in their own lives. While they might help intermittently, especially with grandchildren, the intentionality behind such help is not recognized. Instead, older mothers are often portrayed in the media as being too intrusive, too demanding, or too much in need of being managed, and the emphasis is on the bother they cause others and the care their beleaguered daughters will need to give them in the years to come.

Nevertheless, they continue to engage in the lives of their grown daughters, even though their mothering is different from what it was during the early years. For some, it is fine-tuned and responsive to their daughters' needs and desires, and very much appreciated. For others, it is insensitive, or poorly timed, or irritating, and in the end, rejected by their daughters. But however their mothering is manifested, it remains a significant part of their lives.

Taking Care of Business

When we ask women how they mother now, they most often tell us the tangible things they do for their daughters. Many say they're there to help, whatever their daughters need, and are happy to prepare meals, or pick up grandkids at school, or fold laundry. If their daughters live at a distance, they offer similar assistance when they visit them.

Gloria tells us about helping out Kris in this way. "Every once in a while she'll call and say she needs a break. If I'm free, I'll drive down to San Jose and stay for a day or two, taking care of the tasks that have fallen through the cracks. Lucky for her, I have the energy to do that."

Gloria sees this as her way of mothering, an extension of what she did in the past to ensure her daughter's wellbeing. When we ask if Kris finds her presence in her household intrusive, she laughs. "Are you kidding? She's always liked me taking care of her. That hasn't changed."

Often this kind of hands-on mothering intensifies when there is a crisis. "The hardest period was four years ago, when it became clear that my grandson was in trouble," Gloria says. "He was acting out all over the place, driving everyone nuts. And then my son-in-law was diagnosed with a serious autoimmune disease and had to spend most of his time in bed. Kris asked me to come and help, so I shuttled back and forth from my house to hers for a few months, doing what I could to make things easier for her."

Gloria's son-in-law didn't recover as fast as expected and had to take an unpaid leave from work. Gloria responded—as many mothers do—by helping out financially. "Kris called with the news of his leave, and I could hear in her voice how demoralized she was and frightened about their future. They'd recently gotten word of a rent increase and were scrambling to cover the extra expenses for their son's special program. I wish I could have given her more money, but I'm not rich. I started sending what I could each month, enough for her to feel that there was a little cushion, and I think that helped."

"And now what?" we ask.

"No more money," Gloria says firmly. "Once her husband was able to go back to work, that stopped. The extra money now is going into a fund Judy and I set up for a year's trip to Asia after she retires."

Gloria is able to set limits with her daughter about the amount of hands-on help she provides. As she says, "I give what I can and am happy to do that, but I stop when it isn't needed or if I have other things that are more important. I know women who take on too much and end up becoming resentful. They feel unappreciated by their daughters, or they believe they are taken for granted, or they can't say no. I don't want to be like that."

Gloria is happy to support Kris in many ways, but she tells us about a neighbor who refuses to help her daughter care for her home, possessions, and kids. "My neighbor says it's not her responsibility. She feels that her daughter is a competent adult who makes choices, and if problems emerge, it's up to her to handle them. She raised her to be self-sufficient, and she is not about to change her approach at this point in her life. She's very clear about that."

"What's your opinion about this?" we ask Gloria.

"It's her decision, and I respect that. I'm not that way with Kris, but then, I don't mind doing household chores. I think my neighbor deserves a lot of credit for being truthful about how she feels, even though some people might say she's ungenerous or uncaring. There are lots of ways to be a mother, and she's great at giving her daughter emotional support. That's every bit as important as doing her dishes or babysitting her grandkid."

Offering Emotional Support

When we ask Gloria to give us an example of the emotional support her neighbor gives, she describes a recent incident. "Her daughter was terribly anxious about a new website she was designing for her health-care company; she had been working long hours and nothing seemed to be going right. But when my neighbor looked at a draft of the website, she was really impressed by her daughter's creativity and told her how proud she was and what a great job she was doing. This praise seemed to be just what she needed to persevere and complete the project. My neighbor showed me the website, and she's right, it's terrific. Her daughter just needed that extra bit of support to get through her self-doubt."

Mothers often tell us that providing emotional support is one of the most important ways they help their daughters. It can be as simple as showing an interest in what they're doing and how they're feeling, or making it clear that they are on their daughters' side. Encouragement goes a long way when they are feeling self-doubt, or are overwhelmed, or in need of a shoulder upon which to cry.

Cindy helps out Frida best by reassuring her in those rare times she's doubting herself. "She seems to appreciate it coming from me, at least sometimes," she says. "Frida's so smart, and I always imagine she looks down on me for being such a flake. You wouldn't think she'd accept support from me. But last month when I went to San Francisco and took her out for her birthday, she let it slip that she's under a lot of stress these days balancing work and her family. I could have told her that she's trying to do too much, but she's not able to hear that. Instead I reminded her of how strong she is, how smart she is, and how she has always gotten through whatever is facing her, and how she will once again. I was being the mother she needed in that moment, and she liked it—and boy, did that feel good!"

Emotional support is a natural response for many mothers when their daughters are in trouble. It comes in many forms, depending on the personalities of the women and the parameters of their relationship.

Reassurance is one way of mothering, as we have seen with Cindy. Respectful listening is another. Pat says she's always been a listener. "Terri knows she can call upon me anytime and tell me what's going on, and I'll be able to see things from her point of view." She describes an incident that morning when Terri told her about her feelings toward a woman she met at her pet grooming salon. "There's an attraction there," Pat says, "but when the woman asked Terri to go out for drinks this weekend, she froze. She's still quite ragged from her recent breakup and not sure she's ready to date but really likes this woman. She told me how anxious this situation makes her feels. I listened and let her know I understood, and she found that helpful, as she usually does. Now she'll go ahead and make her own decision about what to do, and whatever it is, I'll support it. That's how it goes with us."

Pat is comfortable listening to Terri as she sorts through the pros and cons of the issues she faces. She's convinced that the best of herself as a mother comes out when she does this. However, we hear from mothers about other ways of being emotionally supportive that go beyond active listening.

Florence feels she helps Harriet best when she serves as a sounding board and gives her constructive feedback. "If she has a problem, or even if she's just considering something, she'll lay it out for me," she says. "I listen carefully, ask questions, and when she's finished I tell her what I think she's saying. Just last night she was struggling with trying to decide what to do about a job offer she received from a nonprofit on the West Coast. One of the benefits would be that she'd move back here, and of course I'd like that, and she would, too. But the more she talked, it became apparent she really loves her current job in Washington, DC, and isn't ready to leave it. I told her that's what I was hearing her say. She thought a little more about it and decided that she'd stay where she is—a smart decision, in my mind, although I admit I was disappointed."

Florence is not able to give constructive feedback to Rhonda, however. "She's always in the midst of a crisis, and the only thing she wants from me is to listen, feel sympathetic about whatever is going on, and be on her side. I do that as best I can and keep my thoughts to myself because I know she needs the support. But that's hard because my impulse is to start to make suggestions, and I can tell you she does not like that. I have the battle scars to prove it."

Advice and Its Discontent

Most mothers like to give advice. Since they've had decades of experience with the vicissitudes of life, they feel confident they can be helpful. It's hard to see their daughters struggling with issues, and they're tempted to come out in full force, suggesting how best to move forward. The reality, however, is that most daughters are not interested in hearing advice from their mothers.

"Rhonda hates it if I get too directive," Florence tells us. "She loses her temper and tells me to stop. Harriet also doesn't like it, and she becomes silent and changes the subject if I talk too much, or says there's no need for me to problem-solve."

Mothers make every effort to support their daughters, understanding that direct advice probably won't be appreciated. But when their daughters make decisions that seem misguided at best and dangerous at worst—like quitting an AA program prematurely, or moving in with an unstable partner, or biking a grandchild through dangerous traffic to day care—they are left concerned that disaster looms ahead. They often don't want to communicate their fear, however, and instead try to support their daughters' autonomy and adulthood rather than give vent to their own anxiety. They are, after all, invested in being emotionally supportive and want at least to try to respect their daughters' decisions.

Pat tells us about her sister, who recently decided to remain silent when her daughter took her to see the house she'd just bought. "My sister was shocked by the state it was in. The porch was falling down, doors were off their hinges, appliances broken, and all her daughter could talk about was how wonderful it would be after the remodel. My sister could have told her it's a terrible mistake to buy such a dump, but she just smiled and congratulated her and wished her many happy years in her new home. She could have added that she hopes she stays out of bankruptcy court because the remodel is going to cost a fortune—but she kept her lips sealed."

Not all women are comfortable keeping their opinions to themselves. It seems wrong not to say what they think when their perspective might avert a disaster or make things better. They're anxious and protective, and can see that their daughters are headed for trouble.

Dolores tells us what happened when she tried to give Yolanda advice while she was in San Antonio a few years ago. "There's already so much tension between us, and I probably should have kept my mouth shut, but one evening my grandsons were all over her, demanding that she take them to McDonald's. I could see that she was exhausted—she had worked all day—and she tried to talk them into staying home, saying she would make their favorite spaghetti dinner instead. But they wouldn't leave her alone and kept hammering at her until I finally said, 'Just tell them no, period. You're the mother, Yolanda, and you need to be in control.' Well, the arguing stopped, but she was furious."

Dolores realizes that her timing was poor and she shouldn't have spoken out in front of the children. But, as she says, that's not who she is. She believes that she was right in her advice, that Yolanda should have the final word with her kids.

"Since then, I try to be more careful with her, but it's hard to keep quiet," she says. "I don't like the way her husband walks all over her and bosses her around, and the boys are taking after him. Yolanda runs to her grandmother, complaining about what's going on, but that doesn't do her any good because her grandmother tells her that's just the way men are and she has to put up with it. If she were to listen to me, I would set her straight about standing up for herself." Dolores sighs. "But that's not going to happen."

"Because?"

"It's that mother-daughter thing. Daughters don't want to hear advice from their mothers." Dolores stops for a moment. "But they can take it from someone else. Vince, my partner, has a grown daughter who lives near me, and I've gotten to know her well and we're really close. She's a single mom, and she drops by sometimes and talks about her problems. I tell her what I think, straight and honest. That doesn't seem to offend her, and often she follows my advice and says it helps. It's sad that I can't be that straightforward with Yolanda."

Every generation has to learn about life in its own way. We interviewed a woman, married for almost fifty years, who told us about her frustration with her daughters recently. As they were sitting over coffee, the topic of marriage arose, and her daughters—one single, the other married—began a lively conversation about its pros and cons. The mother had many insights and suggestions to offer from her own long experience, but whenever she tried to enter the conversation, her remarks were dismissed.

As a nurse, she's not used to being ignored, and her feelings were hurt. But her daughters, who matter most to her in the world, consistently push aside anything she says that sounds like a suggestion. Recently one of her grandchildren seemed to be coming down with a respiratory infection, and when she tried to talk to her daughter about the best way to handle it, her advice went nowhere.

When we ask why she thinks her daughters act this way, she says she suspects it comes from their belief that they know better than she does. They see previous generations—including hers—as being misguided or just plain wrong, and they react to past assumptions with new studies, new revelations, and new understandings. It's up to people in their generation, or so they feel, to correct the mistakes of the past.

This belief is one reason daughters don't want to hear what their mothers think, but it's certainly not the only one. Sometimes there are hidden judgments embedded in mothers' well-meaning advice. No matter how kindly couched, no matter how subtle, there may be a note of condescension, and daughters are sensitive to this. They hear their mothers' advice as judgment on what they're doing or thinking—whether it actually is or not—and they react by turning away. Yet many mothers seem to be unaware that their daughters feel judged by their advice-giving and can't understand why they have such problems with it.

Margo is an astute observer of people's behavior but doesn't notice how patronizing she can be with her own daughter. Her advice, she assures us, comes only from her desire to help Elise get back on track, and she's frustrated because it is not accepted as such. As she says, "There's so much I could do to fix her life, but she won't let me."

She recounts what happened the day before when she ventured into Elise's cottage to drop off a basket of unfolded laundry. "She was huddled on the couch, staring at a sitcom on her computer. 'It's beautiful outside,' I said. 'Don't you want some fresh air? It might energize you if you took a walk. It always does that for me.' Elise answered in a curt tone that she was perfectly fine as she was. A huge wave of impatience rose within me. 'Just trying to help,' I said, as casually as I could. Elise snapped her computer shut and glared at me. 'I don't need your advice, Mom. Why don't you say what you really mean, that I'm not okay like I am. That I should do things like you.'"

Margo was really offended and told Elise that she had misunderstood her good intentions. Back in her house, she went over what had just happened, trying to regain her composure. True, she had been irritated with Elise, but she didn't think she had done anything wrong by suggesting that she get herself together and take a walk. It would be better for her than moping around the cottage in her depressed state. She was sure she had given good advice but didn't recognize that it had come from a place of strong evaluative judgment.

Some mothers are aware that their advice can consciously or unconsciously carry judgment and try to make certain that it is "clean" before they give it. One woman we interviewed, the matriarch of her family, knows that her words carry a lot of weight, and doesn't want her daughter to feel worse because of something she says without thinking carefully about it first. When we ask how she goes about giving advice, she assures us that she doesn't offer it very often, but if she has a suggestion to make, she asks her daughter first if she wants to hear it. Sometimes the daughter says no, she can sort through the matter herself. But if the response is yes, the mother knows she's bought into listening and her advice will be welcomed.

She tells us that her daughter has been most receptive to her guidance at those times when she has been going through stages that her mother herself experienced, like having her first child and entering menopause. Then her motherly expertise and direction was most appreciated. But, she reminds us, her advice has never been seen as the final answer to all her daughter's questions, but as one resource among many. Her daughter, like others in her generation, lives in a world where she is bombarded with instructions from books, the Internet, and friends, and is used to weighing the options and choosing among them.

Maintaining Family Ties

Another of the many ways that women continue to actively mother is by helping their daughters remain connected to the larger family. In this age of too many responsibilities and not enough time, daughters can easily lose track of people who are important to them.

"I'm the one who knows what's going on with everyone," Florence tells us. "Our extended family is spread all over the map, and Harriet and Rhonda can't keep up. Yet they want to stay in touch, so they do that through me. I filter the news and give them the headlines, and I pass on the details of their lives. Harriet especially appreciates my efforts because she's such a family person."

Florence is the matriarch, the connecting link, the glue in

the family. She manages to get everyone together for important holiday celebrations. As she says, "I start talking to my kids early in September about Thanksgiving. That gets the ball rolling. Sometimes they complain that it's way too early to make plans, but I know they appreciate my efforts because the holiday is special for all of us and won't get organized unless I do it. Sometimes we have thirty or forty people here at my house. Harriet flies in from the East Coast and my other kids and grandkids come, and my sisters and their kids and grandkids, and an uncle in his nineties, and there are usually a few others who don't have a place to go."

Mothers are likely to be the holders of family tradition, the bearers of continuity. They are the elders, the ones who know everybody and everything that happened in the past. They bring a larger perspective to their daughters' lives.

Florence tells us about a time when Rhonda was upset about a man she was dating. "She had been hoping they'd end up marrying but had just found out that he already had a wife and a baby. She knew she should break off with him right away but couldn't do it. She felt like she was in molasses, unable to move forward. I told her about her aunt, who had been in a similar situation many years ago. She too had been stuck for a while, unable to move, wanting to believe the man's promises, but she finally was able to let the relationship go. My daughter felt reassured by this because she saw her love for a married man in a larger light and became more confident that she'd get to the other side of it."

Florence believes that another part of mothering is keeping her daughters connected to their past. She often reminds them of things they did, but is careful not to bring up the troubled times when Rhonda experimented with drugs or ran away as a teenager. As Florence says, "It's too easy for my still-raw feelings about those episodes to emerge, so I return to the early memories, like the way she used to dance around the living room pretending to be a Supreme. Recently, while she was here, she did this thing of unconsciously pulling at her hair, just like she used to do, and I remarked on it. I think she likes to hear these stories about her past because they connect her with the present."

Florence is keenly aware of her role as the center of her family and realizes she needs to navigate carefully. "I know women who make a mess," she tells us. "They gossip about one family member to another or reveal a confidence their daughter has told them, or get in the middle of arguments. Then everybody gets mad at them."

Mothers often insist on maintaining family ties even when they are complicated. There are usually less favored or troubled relatives who get folded into the ongoing life of the family one way or another. But trickiest of all is the question of how to relate to ex-husbands or partners who are the fathers of their daughters.

For some mothers, the answer to this question is obvious because their exes are not around. Nobody knows anymore where Dolores's ex-husband is or what he's doing, and the family goes on as though he doesn't exist. Cindy's ex-husband moved to England after their divorce and still lives there, painting and teaching art. Every few years he comes to the Bay Area to see Frida, but Cindy has no contact with him. She is fine with this because she believes that people should go their separate ways after a divorce. However, if it were important to

Frida to bring her parents together again, she'd honor that because she no longer has hostile feelings toward him. And she's curious about what he's like after all these years.

Pat's situation is more complicated because her ex-husband lives twenty-five miles away with his second family. After the divorce they didn't see each other, but about five years ago Terri started to talk about bringing them all together for a visit. As Pat tells it, "Her partner at that time came from a family where everyone was invited to celebrations, even after divorces or breakups, and she said something to Terri about how strange it was that her parents didn't socialize." Pat rolls her eyes. "Hey, I liked it the way it was before, never seeing him or his wife. But Terri and her partner invited all of us over to their apartment for dinner one night. I didn't want to go, but of course I felt I had to. It actually wasn't too bad, and Terri seemed so thrilled to have us all together. My ex-husband's wife is a pleasant enough woman, and we found plenty to talk about since she also loves animals. Their son just graduated from college and seems like a good kid. My ex is still the operator he always has been, but guess what? His wife has to deal with him, not me."

"Do you see them very often now?"

"Sometimes on holidays or birthdays. Getting together means a lot to Terri, and I'm glad to do that for her. I've gotten used to being with them, and I'm past being angry at my ex, although every once in a while I remember something horrible he did like refusing to give Terri a loan to help her start her business. But I remind myself that was the past, and the important thing is to mend those bridges for my daughter's sake."

Pat has come to accept spending time with her ex-husband

and his family, but Gloria feels differently about the situation. "I wish my ex-husband and his wife would just disappear," she says. "I can't help it, the situation is so irritating. After our divorce I never saw them except from a distance at school graduations and athletic events, and I just ignored them. But in recent years, we've been face to face a few times."

The first meeting was not planned. "Leanne was in town, staying with her dad as usual, and she called and asked if I wanted to go to dinner with her. It was a freezing, rainy night, and I told her I'd pick her up because she didn't have a car. When I got to her dad's house at the appointed hour, I texted her to let her know I was there, but no answer. I should have waited outside, but I went to the door and rang the bell, and my ex and his wife answered it with martinis in hand. They asked me in and said Leanne would be right down, but she didn't appear for at least ten minutes. The three of us hemmed and hawed at each other all that time. It was horrible."

Gloria was angry that she had been thrust into this situation, and when she and her daughter got to the car, she asked her why she had left them alone for so long. "Leanne answered that I was an adult and could handle it, and besides, it was time that we all got to be friendlier. Needless to say, I didn't like the idea," Gloria tells us. "And then several months later Leanne invited Judy and me and Kris and her family to celebrate the Fourth of July together at her father's house. She said it would be a big family party with ribs cooked on the outdoor grill and swimming in their fancy Olympic pool. I was set to say no, but Kris told me she was going and Judy chided me for being so negative, so I agreed."

Gloria gives us a disgusted look. "What a mistake. Nobody

had a good time, not even Judy, who gets along with everyone and is the nicest person in the world. Afterward she and I agreed that we'd never do that again. The following year, both Leanne and Kris approached me, saying they wanted to get all of us together at their dad's house again on July Fourth, but this time I said count me out. I'm sure my daughters didn't like that, but why go through the motions of being a family if everyone feels uncomfortable and awkward? The truth is that their dad and I got divorced almost forty years ago, and they've lived with it all this time. There are lots of things in this world that need fixing, like poverty and injustice, but this isn't one of them."

Accompanying Daughters

Much of the time mothers are present with their daughters in a sort of accompanying way. "When I'm with Frida, I'm just there," Cindy says. "How do you explain that?"

"Mothering doesn't always have to be instrumental," we say.

It's easy to talk about mothering when specific activities are described, but when mothers accompany their daughters, it's more complicated to explain. For many, this is the state they say they're in most of the time.

"I'm the mother, and she's the daughter," Cindy says. "That never changes."

"And when you're accompanying her, you aren't actively mothering, but it's always a possibility."

"That happened when I took Frida out for her birthday and

ended up reassuring her," Cindy replies. "I never expected that."

"Specific acts of mothering come and go," we say. "But it's always a possibility when the two of you are together, because of who you are to each other."

The mother-daughter relationship is unique, and many mothers say they love to be in the presence of their daughters, side by side. They feel comfortable and appreciative of the opportunity to experience the flowering of their relationship, as they sometimes call it. And when they shift into helping or supporting them, they draw from the goodwill that exists between them and the many hours spent together in this way.

Modeling the Years Ahead

The daughters of the women we interview are middle-aged and becoming more conscious of their own aging. At the halfway point of their lives, they are going through menopause or on the other side of it, and their children are growing older. When they look in the mirror, they notice that lines are appearing on their faces, their hair is graying, their bodies changing.

Many mothers tell us that their daughters look to them as models for the years to come. They're curious about the changes in their mothers' bodies and want to know more about the ailments or diseases they've had in the last decades. They might ask questions or simply notice from afar, but the genetic connection can't be ignored, and daughters anticipate that their years ahead will be affected at least to some extent by what they have inherited. They're interested also in how their mothers handle the emotional challenges of growing older, their moods and attitudes. Some seem determined to do everything differently so they don't end up like them, but others use them as models for aging in a healthy, constructive way.

One mother who has struggled with back issues for the last twenty years tells us that she feels it's important to model a positive approach to aging for her daughter. "It's what I can give her," she says. "She lives in New Hampshire and we don't see each other much, but I know she tracks how I'm doing. I take good care of myself and make sure to continue seeing friends, going to recitals and concerts, and volunteering. I easily could get depressed by my condition and stay in my apartment all the time, but I don't want that. My own mother withdrew from life in her sixties and stopped watching her diet and exercising, and I vowed never to be that way. I want my daughter to see me as a competent, involved person, an example of how to grow old. I like to think that she'll remember me this way after I'm gone."

Florence talks about the line of women in her family and how much she was affected by her own mother. "My mother lived into her nineties, taking care of others and opening her home to whoever needed it until the end. She was my model, a strong woman who never bowed down to adversity. I learned so much from her, and even today I think of what she would say or do."

"Are you a model like that to your daughters?" we ask.

"In many ways," Florence says. "Harriet naturally patterns herself after me because we're so similar and so close, but it's more complicated with Rhonda. I know she resists certain things about me, but sometimes I'll see her watching me, taking in how I'm handling this or that, and she'll ask about it. Recently my arthritis has been acting up and it's hard for me to reach high kitchen cabinets, so I've taken to stacking plates and cups on a table below. I was making sandwiches for the two of us the other day, and she asked why I was doing this. I told her getting old means making a lot of compromises, but you just have to roll with them and save your energy. I think she heard that."

When Daughters Need Special Help

Women typically tell us that their time, energy, and resources go to their daughters in smaller amounts now than they did when they were younger. But this lightness in mothering is not possible for one group of mothers, those with daughters who are in trouble and dependent on them. The demands on them as mothers can be at least as intense as they were in past years.

Sometimes this situation is temporary, as when a daughter has a health crisis and her mother puts everything aside to care for her. As frightening and difficult as that can be, it's not a longstanding arrangement. But when daughters are physically or mentally unable to take care of themselves, and there are no other resources, the burden rests on the mother with no end in sight.

Margo expresses her thoughts about this. "I thought I'd signed up for an eighteen-year package, but oh, was I wrong. When Elise went off to college, I assumed the mothering business with her was over, but she dropped out and came home. Like a boomerang. I hoped she'd eventually become independent, but that has never happened. Sure, there were some years when she lived with various friends, or guys she met, but nothing lasted. Before my grandson was born, she worked at a bookstore, but that came to an end when the store was sold, and she has become increasingly nonfunctional since then. For the past five years she's been in that cottage, dependent on us, and I can't see how that will ever change."

Margo's pain is palpable and she feels the strain of living in such close proximity to her daughter. Although her mothering efforts are often rebuffed, she makes sure there is food in the refrigerator, the heater is working, and her grandson has the clothing and school supplies he needs. She carefully watches over her daughter but also tries to keep her own life on track by scheduling clients, friends, and activities back-to-back. "I'm the busiest person I know," she says. "But I have to be. Otherwise, I'd be filled with so much despair that I'd fall apart myself."

Margo, with her speeded-up life, is unlike a woman we interviewed whose daily existence revolves around her middle-aged schizophrenic daughter, diagnosed when she was twenty. The years since then have included hospitalizations and stays in halfway houses, but her illness has been managed primarily at home. Since she can't be left alone, this requires her mother to be present full time. Recently her daughter moved into a halfway living situation, and daily life is a bit easier, but she still watches very carefully, phoning her several times a day, checking up on her. She says she can't allow herself to become complacent about her condition because it changes so fast, and she knows all the little signs that she is getting worse and needs to be hospitalized.

Yet when she talks about her daughter, she is surprisingly upbeat, saying that despite all the troubles, she couldn't ask for a more wonderful daughter. When she's well, she's intelligent, loving, and interested in hearing everything the mother is doing, and she remembers it all. In some ways she is like a best friend. Even when the daughter gets sick, there is never nastiness, just craziness.

She says that she's closer to her daughter than just about anyone else. She brings goodness into her life, and in some ways has been her spiritual teacher. While the mother remembers being impatient and irritable earlier in her life, she knows she can't behave in those ways with her vulnerable daughter and consequently has become more compassionate and loving.

It's very moving to hear this woman speak with so much appreciation about her mentally ill daughter. She is unusual, however, in her positive attitude. We've spoken with others who resent the time and energy they must put into them or the money they spend on their care. They did not expect to have to do this at their age, but there is no one else to carry the load.

When daughters break down or are in trouble, they may need a period of intensive mothering before they find their way forward. Another woman we interviewed calls this "redemptive mothering." After her daughter lost her job and fell apart, the mother, realizing that she needed to heal from her wounds, took her into her home, cared for her as she had when she was little, and listened for long hours to her sorrow. One root of her daughter's problems, the mother believed, was a lot of anger toward her for divorcing her dad and never putting her first. She listened carefully as this painful history was spoken and did her best not to become defensive. Slowly the daughter has gotten better, and is now living on her own and volunteering with troubled teens. And the mother has been given the gift of being able to repair her mothering from the past. As she says, it was a matter of finding the right approach and giving it time.

Sometimes mothers return to the parenting business because they are responsible full time for their grandchildren. One tells us that her preteen granddaughter lives with her during the school year because her daughter has taken a job in another state and can't provide consistent supervision. The girl is becoming a little wild, and she worries that she won't be able to control her as she grows older. She says full-time care is hard at her age, and she's envious of the freedom her friends have, although she loves her granddaughter. But somebody has to take care of the girl, and there isn't anyone but her.

Some mothers talk about the complexity of living in three-generation households with their daughters and grandkids. We hear about the sweet moments and the pleasures of having intimate contact with loved ones, and we also hear about the times of dissention, the issues of boundaries, the loss of independence, and the tasks that must be done—the cooking, laundry, and cleaning, picking up kids after school or watching over them.

Intensive mothering—whether it be watching over a troubled or sick daughter or taking care of a grandchild full time—can be overwhelming for aging women, at least partly because it was not anticipated. When their children were young, they expected to give themselves over to mothering them for a certain number of years and then letting them go, and after that they assumed they'd have the rest of their lives without full-time responsibility. There's a feeling of shock and disorientation among women we meet who have returned to concentrated mothering.

A child-centered focus takes its toll. No matter how

healthy mothers are, no matter how much they've kept themselves in shape, the reality is that they are older women now. They are less energetic and become tired more easily, and they can't juggle all the things they did in the past.

Still, many mothers step forward to take on this responsibility when it is required. Some are angry about it, some exhausted, some loving and appreciative of the opportunity to help—but they do it because they care deeply about their troubled daughters or their dependent grandchildren. They worry about what's going to happen to them when they no longer are around. It's frightening to think that these offspring will be left alone, without their support, and unable to fend for themselves. That's the worst nightmare, one mother tells us—then she adds that she'll just have to defy nature and keep on living.

Estranged Daughters

We have interviewed a few mothers who are completely alienated from their daughters. But even when this is the painful reality, their daughters are not forgotten. Letters, birthday cards, and even little gifts might be sent—whether they are opened is another matter—and words of greeting or concern have been passed on to them. These mothers say that they hold their daughters in their hearts, even though there is no contact and even though they are deeply hurt by their rejection.

Still, there is always hope. As one estranged mother says, her mothering now is limited to silent well-wishes, but you never can know what will happen in the future. Perhaps a time will come when her daughter returns to her, wanting to talk. It has happened before.

But some daughters never return. One woman has not seen her daughter for sixteen years, and her way of mothering her, she says, is to let her go. She realizes this sounds contradictory—shouldn't a mother hold on to her child?—but she has come to accept that this separation is best for her daughter, even though she does not understand why it is necessary. The most loving thing she can do, she believes, is to cut all ties and sadly bless her daughter as she goes on her way.

A Work in Progress

Relationships are never static. Daughters' priorities and circumstances can change abruptly, without notice, and mothers are called upon to be flexible in response. Likewise, daughters' moods shift, and what they find helpful one day is irritating to them the next. Mothers feel that they are scrambling to find successful ways to support and help these unpredictable but beloved offspring.

Cindy often feels confused by the quick changes of mood in Frida. "When I took her out for her birthday last month and she told me how stressed she was with her job and family, she seemed to appreciate my reassurance. But last night I phoned her, and it was as though we'd never had that conversation. I asked if she's still under a lot of stress, and she acted offended. 'What stress? I'm fine, why ask me that?' she snapped. I thought I was doing something helpful by bringing up this subject, but obviously I wasn't."

"Why do you think she responded that way?" we ask.

"I suppose she likes to be in charge of bringing up the hard things, or maybe she didn't want to think about stress in that moment or was embarrassed by having let down her guard with me last month. I don't know. I can run rings around myself trying to figure out what she's thinking when I make a mistake like that, but I just back up, try to smooth it over, and leave the subject alone."

Mothers would like the satisfaction of knowing that their efforts are appreciated and mean something to their daughters. But often that doesn't happen. Daughters are too busy or too engrossed in their own problems to give them this assurance, or the thought simply does not cross their minds. Or the unresolved feelings from the past make it impossible for daughters to recognize what they are receiving. Mothering, then, becomes a gesture outwards, a gift that is given without acknowledgement.

When mothering is going well, it brings a great deal of satisfaction to women. They are wrapping up their years as mothers in ways that feel right to them. As Pat says, "Being a mother is the most important thing I'm doing now. I make mistakes, and we have problems sometimes, but I do my best."

Pat, like every other mother, does not have the perfect formula for mothering her midlife daughter. Sometimes she says the wrong thing or fails to be there for Terri when she is needed. Problems arise between them, as they do in any intimate relationship. "When that happens, we struggle through, like everyone else," she says. "I guess that's the way it will always be. Mothering never ends."

CHAPTER FIVE

Navigating the Difficulties

⁓

Imagine mothers and daughters existing without a care, moving through time in perfect harmony. The vision may be inspiring, but it's not reality. The mothers we know say they sometimes experience anger and misunderstanding, feelings of competition and envy, differing expectations and desires, and struggles over boundaries. Even those who are very close to their daughters can recount moments, if not months or years, when the balance between them was disrupted and their bond felt at least somewhat compromised.

Mothers talk often about the hard times they've had with their daughters. Because of the complex, primal nature of the connection and the layers of history that exist, difficulties inevitably arise, often without warning. Whether these times are described as short-lived or long-lasting, they are upsetting and significant.

The question is not whether difficulties exist but how they are navigated. Through the years mothers have developed ways to get along with others, and many of their rough edges have been rubbed off and their unrealistic expectations whittled down. But this does not mean that they sail easily through the issues that arise with their daughters. They're often overwhelmed by feelings that confuse and confound them, and they don't know how to heal what has gone wrong. The situation is intensified by their desire to be close to their daughters and their fear that the bond between them might be broken.

Angry Daughters

Issues of anger are mentioned most often by mothers as difficult to navigate. Anger is an obvious emotion: it comes in bold colors and dramatic strokes and makes itself known by disgusted looks, impatient sighs, harsh words, or icy withdrawal. Mothers are very aware of its presence, perhaps because it is so disruptive in the relationship if left unaddressed.

Mothers feel apprehensive when their daughters get angry at them. The emotion can come as a flash, arising unexpectedly, or the surfacing of a long-standing issue, or another round in a conflict that fails to be resolved. However it emerges, its existence causes mothers to feel defensive, unsettled, frightened, and sometimes angry in return.

As Florence says, "I'm used to managing conflict in the community and at the university, but when Rhonda gets angry at me, it's a different matter. Recently we were visiting on the phone, enjoying ourselves, but I made a comment she took as a criticism. She became quiet for a minute and then exploded, saying she's sick and tired of hearing about her deficits. I was shocked because I hadn't said anything that was critical of her. I tried to defend myself, but she slammed down the phone."

After the conversation ended, Florence sat at her kitchen

table, trying to eat lunch, but she couldn't stop ruminating about what had happened with Rhonda and considered calling her back to explain what she had meant to say. She had a whole speech prepared in her mind. But then her thoughts shifted to her son's fiftieth birthday party that was planned to take place at her home the following Sunday. She very much wanted Rhonda to be there; perhaps it would help to ease the tension between her and her brother.

Florence continues, "I felt I had to do something about the situation. I could argue with Rhonda about hanging up on me, but I was afraid that would make things worse and she'd refuse to come to the birthday party. She can be that way. Or I could apologize to her and smooth things over. I waited a few more hours then called and said I was sorry I had offended her; it had not been my intention. She accepted my apology, and that was that. We began to talk about what I was cooking for the birthday party on Sunday as though nothing had happened."

We asked Florence how she managed to set her anger at Rhonda aside so easily. "I've learned a thing or two in my life," she says. "I can see the long view. I cared more about making peace with Rhonda and getting her to the party than telling her how angry I was."

"So it was a tradeoff?"

"At my age I don't need to say every angry word in my mind," she answers. "I can be the adult in this relationship. Rhonda has a lot of issues, and I don't want to get caught up in her stuff."

Florence is not alone in stepping away from her angry feelings in the service of making peace. Pat, too, has become an expert in doing this.

"Terri gets irritable and turns on me," Pat says. "I do everything I can to please her, but it doesn't always work. Recently I stopped by her apartment with a cactus plant I'd bought for her. I thought she'd love it because it's in a bright blue Mexican pot and she likes that sort of thing, but when she came to the door, I could see she was in a bad mood. 'Why are you here?' she frowned, and when I gave her the plant, she muttered a few words of thanks but didn't invite me in. She was treating me like an unwelcome stranger after I'd done something nice for her, and I felt hurt by that."

"Did you tell her?"

"I just left. I stayed away from her for a few days until she came around. I try not to take it personally when this kind of thing happens. Nobody's perfect. When I was Terri's age, I used to be mean to my own mom sometimes, but she didn't get bothered. She was able to rise above whatever I did, and I'm trying to do that with Terri. I don't want to fight with her."

Deflect, diffuse, and distract. These are the primary responses mothers tell us they use to manage their daughters' anger. Even though a few say they engage when their daughters strike out at them, most are very much more careful. They couch their language, swallow their feelings, and do their best to smooth over tensions. They "let things settle" and "find the right moment" to approach their daughters because, for many, excavating the roots of their daughters' anger is too fraught with the possibility of losing them.

There are, however, some mothers and daughters who are able to have honest conversations when anger arises. One woman tells us that she makes sure to ask her daughter what is going on if she senses any tension. She's willing to stop everything and listen to her complaint in a non-defensive way because she believes that's the best path to resolving their issues. It works sometimes, she tells us. Not always. The majority of mothers respond as Pat does, however. They are more concerned about staying connected to their daughters and fear disrupting the status quo, even if it is punctuated by bouts of anger.

Mothers' Anger at Daughters

Mothers generally are uneasy about expressing angry feelings directly to their daughters because they want to be "good" mothers, loving and supportive. They tamp down their irritation and give their offspring more leeway to express their negative feelings than they give themselves.

When we ask mothers what their daughters do that riles them the most, they often describe those times when a pleasing conversation is twisted into a confrontation and their words are taken out of context and thought to mean something different from what they intend. Or when the past seems to hold great sway, causing their daughters to see the present through the eyes of the trauma they experienced as children.

Dolores's relationship with Yolanda is marked by this frustrating dynamic. "How long do I have to dance around our history?" she asks. "For me, the past is the past, but Yolanda still holds on to it. A few days ago I called her—it was a miracle she had the time to talk—and I was telling her that I was supervising the remodel of the lobby at the apartment building I manage. There's a lot to do with ordering new carpet and so forth. But this somehow reminded her of living with me in Oakland and when I had her bedroom repainted without asking her. She said how traumatic that had been and how that incident had been one more reason why she lost her trust in me. Oh my god! I listened to her and said I was sorry that had happened, but inside I was seething. I had just wanted to tell her what I was doing and have her know a little more about me."

It's frustrating for mothers when the past intervenes and they are misunderstood or reminded of the ways they failed. Likewise, when daughters are floundering because of poor life choices, addiction issues, or mental health limitations, mothers may be sympathetic but become impatient and annoyed at the demands their daughters' lives make on them.

"I have to admit it," Margo says. "I am constantly irritated at Elise for not being more together. I try to be understanding, but I can't pull it off. When I go into that cottage and see the chaos around her, I want to scream."

"How do you handle your anger?" we ask.

"I push it down inside me, and grin and bear it. What are my choices?"

Margo goes on to tell us about a friend of hers who lives with even more frustration than she does. "This woman has twin grandsons with behavioral problems living in her home because her daughter is unable to care for them. At least Elise manages to do the basics for my grandson, and he's a joy to all of us."

Margo's friend lives with her eight-year-old twin grandsons who moved in with her after her daughter remarried. "Her new husband did not want the children around and told my friend's daughter that she had to choose between him and the boys. She chose him," Margo says. "There was nowhere else for the boys to go except to my friend's home. She's furious with her daughter for abdicating her responsibility as a mother, and she calls the new husband a monster. Her anger extends to the jittery, demanding twins, although she tries hard to keep it hidden. It's not their fault they ended up in her care, but they can't sit still for a minute and they fight nonstop and demand too much from her. Her home, which used to be so peaceful and quiet, has been turned upside down."

We ask Margo if her friend has talked to her daughter about how hard this situation is on her. "She's skirted around it," Margo answers, "but her daughter is already depressed and anxious, and she feels it would be too much of a stress on her if she complains. She's choosing to be there for her and the kids for now."

We ask if Margo's friend is concerned that her anger at her daughter might seep out at an unguarded moment. Margo says it probably won't. "She knows how to control herself, and she's strong—stronger than her daughter—and skilled at concealment. In the future, when she and her daughter are on the other side of all this, the subject might come up, but she doesn't have a great need for her to know how she feels right now. Her need is for all of them to get through this crisis and to the other side, whatever that might be."

Mothers generally want to help their daughters, but they often become angry when their efforts are not acknowledged or appreciated. Many say the lack of gratitude makes them feel invisible and taken for granted, which upsets them more than any other interaction.

We interviewed a woman who recently sold her floral

design business, and her daughter asked if she'd take care of her German Shepherd while she went on vacation for three weeks. The mother agreed because she had more free time, and was easily able to feed and walk the dog twice a day. When the dog cut his leg on barbed wire, she took him to the vet and made sure his shots were up to date, and tended to his wound after she brought him home. She didn't really mind all the extra caretaking, but when her daughter returned, there was barely a word of thanks. The mother was angry and hurt about her lack of gratitude but didn't say anything. When we asked her why, she said it would have been humiliating to have to ask for thanks.

Afterwards she thought a lot about what had transpired between herself and her daughter. When she was honest with herself, she realized that one of the reasons she had agreed to care for the dog was to please her daughter and be the "good mama," deserving of praise and a pat on the back. Her daughter had no way of knowing these were her hopes. The mother decided she's not going to have hidden expectations like that again. It isn't good for her, and in the end, it's not good for her daughter.

Many mothers shy away from expressing anger at their grown daughters, whatever the issue. The price is too high if something goes wrong: daughters might be hurt, or withdraw, or attack back, or the relationship can be broken. Since daughters are so important to their mothers, and the relationship is such a source of meaning in their lives as they age, they want to do everything possible to avoid these painful outcomes.

The belief exists in our post-Freudian culture that unexpressed anger is toxic and can lead to physical or emotional damage, but these mothers don't seem to be concerned about the results of concealing their strong feelings. It's more important to them to make sure that nothing damages their relationships or their daughters. This takes priority over giving vent to their feelings.

Mothers who don't directly express their anger often say they write in their journals or talk with their husbands, partners, or friends, making sure to find safe places to let off steam. In this way their anger becomes less of a burden, and they often end up with a broader perspective on the situation.

But not all women handle anger by holding it in. A few we've interviewed create a time to sit and talk with their daughters when there is tension, identifying what they need to work through to resolve it. They say what is in their hearts and listen with openness to their daughters. They can then let the angry interaction move into the past and be put to rest. In these relationships unresolved anger and tensions never build up because everything can be said and received with care and respect.

Mothers from cultural backgrounds or families where anger is a much more accepted and ordinary part of life tell us that they have no problem with loud words or big feelings. They just say whatever it is, not in a way that would be hurtful, but to let the other person know how they feel. That person might argue back, and the fight might go on for a while, but its existence is not considered an issue. The relationship rolls on in a generally satisfying way with periodic bouts of passionate argument.

Other mothers don't want to let issues fester with their daughters but are uncomfortable with full-out angry exchanges and try to find a middle ground. As one told us, it doesn't work to lose her temper with her daughter, because she withdraws, so she appeals to her as a reasonable person. She tells us about a time when her daughter arrived an hour late to pick up her toddler after hours of babysitting and didn't give her a reason or even apologize. The mother was fuming but said in a calm voice, "I'm happy to take care of the baby, but in the future you have to be back on time. I missed my yoga class tonight." That was all she said, but her daughter got the point. And the mother's anger at her lessened.

When Daughters Reject Mothers

The most heartbreaking experience of all for many women is being rejected by their daughters. Whether it be a slight that nobody else notices or a refusal to connect or communicate, rejection leaves mothers feeling bruised, disappointed, confused, and angry.

One mother tells us that she feels rejected because her daughter won't participate in the family's tradition of Sunday dinners. Several relatives gather together for these dinners, and she is deeply attached to them because they provide an important sense of continuity. The interactions have not always been simple, yet the commitment to be together for a few hours a week has bound the generations together during the hard times.

But her daughter is utterly uninterested in this tradition. The few times she appeared in recent years were a grave disappointment because she was restless and resentful. Her mother, as the prime organizer of these dinners, felt rejected by her attitude, even though she understands that not everyone likes weekly visits with relatives. She says she tries not to take it personally, but in her heart of hearts, she feels that if her daughter really loved her, she would be there in good humor with them at least sometimes on Sundays.

Mothers often tell us that they sense they are less important or interesting to their daughters than the other people in their lives, and this makes them feel rejected. They're slipped in at the last minute, or engagements with them are broken, or they don't fit into their daughters' schedules.

Cindy feels that Frida treats her in this way. "She only finds time to talk if there's nothing more important going on, which doesn't happen often," she tells us. "She's completely involved with her husband and kids. I know that's reasonable and appropriate, but I can't help but feel left out. I'll get an invitation for holidays and sometimes for birthdays, but that's about it. I appear with her husband's parents, we eat dinner sitting around their rosewood table and chat politely, and then we leave. It seems like I can't get into the inner circle of that family. When I ask Frida if they'd like to come up to Petaluma and spend an afternoon with me, there is always some excuse. I understand, sort of. But I feel terribly left out."

Cindy goes on to say that even though Frida doesn't want much contact with her, she thinks her two teenaged granddaughters would appreciate seeing her more often. "The youngest one, especially, has a lot of artistic talent and a personality more like mine, and I'd love to get her and her sister into my studio, playing around with paint and all the fun stuff I have. But that never happens. Probably Frida's afraid I'd be a bad influence on them. It's too bad because the girls now are busier than ever, and they'll soon go off to college."

Mothers do not like being disregarded or their hard-won wisdom ignored. One mother we interviewed worked in the field of child development for twenty-five years and has a storehouse of information to offer her daughter as she raises her children. But if she tries to share it, her daughter abruptly turns away or changes the subject. The mother says she understands why she does this—daughters don't like being instructed by their mothers—but the rejecting way in which she turns away cuts her to the core.

Mothers react in different ways to such perhaps inadvertent or inevitable slights. Some feel hurt or angry, although they usually are careful to contain those feelings for fear of making the situation even more awkward and unsatisfying than it already is. Others express disappointment in their daughter's priorities. But whatever their response is to the slight, they all express a sense of rejection and loss.

Some who feel rejected by their daughters find relief with their grandchildren, assuming they are allowed access to them. As Margo tells us, "I have a great relationship with my grandson. He often sleeps in our house, and I lie down next to him and snuggle and we read stories together and talk. The sweetness of being with him helps to balance the sourness that comes from Elise."

Another colleague has a granddaughter in her early twenties who lives close by. After an explosive argument a year ago, her daughter cut off all connection, but the granddaughter checks up on her and is very loving. She feels she has lost her daughter, at least for now, but is fortunate to have such an attentive grandchild. It's not the same—she misses her daughter terribly and hopes they'll reunite—but the girl's presence is a gift.

Some mothers have no hope at all of healing the estrangement and rejection that has taken place. We interviewed a woman who says she lost her daughter in the 1990s during the period when therapists were hypersensitive to issues of sexual abuse and pushed patients to dig for memories. The daughter became certain that she'd been violated and broke off all contact with her mother, accusing her of not protecting her from harm. Even after repeated attempts by the mother to talk to her and try to understand why she thought this, the daughter refused to see her. That was nineteen years and eleven months ago, and the situation hasn't changed. As the mother tells us, this is the most excruciatingly painful thing that has happened in her life. And there is nothing she can do about it.

Mother's Rejecting Feelings

Popular literature labels mothers who act in rejecting ways toward their daughters as withholding, narcissistic, or punitive. This judgment is typically applied to the most extreme of cases—those mothers who never bond with their infants or those who are unusually cruel—but it also is used for occasional moments of rejection. The societal verdict is clear: motherly rejection is a sign of moral failure or mental illness.

But what mother doesn't sometimes reject her daughter or have strong judgmental feelings? These feelings are as much a part of life as others, yet mothers fear them and are ashamed when they arise. Sometimes rejection is considered to be so destructive that it becomes submerged and is often not even acknowledged by the mothers themselves.

We had a conversation recently with a church-going mother whose daughter has completely rejected her religion. She tells us that she can't accept her daughter because of this, and their visits are tense because of her unwillingness to change. As the years pass, they see less of each other, and the gap between them is growing. When we ask how she deals with her feelings of rejection toward her daughter, she looks at us in a puzzled way. "Rejection? Perhaps I'm judgmental once in a while, but no, I don't reject her. I love her."

Other mothers are more aware of their rejecting feelings. Gloria tells us that she found herself wanting to avoid being with Leanne when she was in town recently. "She called, saying she was free that evening, and asked if she could drop by. I had no other plans, but I told her that it wouldn't work, sorry. My response wasn't from anger, but I had a sudden hardness toward her. I just didn't want to be with her."

"Do you think she sensed it?" we ask.

"I don't know. She seemed a little surprised."

"Did that bother you?"

"I don't like feeling rejecting toward my child. Even though we've had problems over the years, I want to be there for her, especially when she reaches out to me. But in that moment I felt myself retract."

Gloria goes on to tell us that she talked at length with Judy about what had happened with Leanne. "In her opinion, I shouldn't feel ashamed of how I felt because Leanne so often has not treated me well. I countered by saying that I'm still her mother and want to be welcoming to her. Judy asked me why the feeling of rejection is so hard for me to have, and we began to talk about how painful it had been for me as a child when my father pushed me away after my mother died. I was just ten, and his response was a huge blow. Judy pointed out that the two situations are entirely different. Back then, I was motherless and desperately in need of his love and support, and his abuse just about destroyed me, but Leanne is an adult and I almost always treat her in a supportive way. Maybe that evening I didn't want to be with her, but that's not the same as what I experienced as a child. She reminded me that I've done everything I can through the years to accept and love her, even though it's been very hard because of her negativity toward me."

"Did you still feel ashamed after what Judy said?"

"I agreed with her perspective, but guilt doesn't go away that easily."

Rejection comes in many forms. A few mothers acknowledge that these feelings have been dominant throughout the entire relationship, and even though they've tried not to act on them, they don't seem to diminish. Sometimes they exist because their daughters display a painful mirror image of qualities they have tried to excise from themselves, such as being too submissive or too impulsive. But with most mothers, rejecting feelings appear every so often in relationships that are basically loving, and they're centered on certain concerns.

One of the most frequently mentioned reasons for having rejecting feelings is the way daughters take care of themselves, their homes, or their children. A mother who used to be a model says that her daughter has let herself go, and this is affecting their relationship. Whenever the mother sees her, she can hardly control herself. *Get a haircut*, she wants to say. *Stop wearing those frayed pants and ugly tops. Go to the gym and lose thirty pounds.* She'd be happy to take her daughter on a shopping trip to get a new wardrobe, but whenever she suggests it, the answer is no. The mother fears that she will ruin what has been a good relationship by the rejecting feelings that overwhelm her every time she sees her daughter, and she tries to keep her tone positive and not let her judgment show.

Mothers also feel rejecting toward their daughters because of the life choices they have made. One we interviewed has a daughter who has been unhappily married for twelve years to a man who has serious anger issues toward authority figures. He can't keep a job because he lashes out at his bosses and won't apologize, so her daughter has to support him. The mother is disgusted that she puts up with this situation and discouraged about the possibility of any change.

When we ask her how she handles these negative feelings, she tells us that she tries to keep in mind the other ways her daughter is successful. Her marriage might be a disaster, but she is an intelligent, creative woman who succeeds in her job as an art teacher, and she holds the same values of responsibility and decency that the mother does. She's now in her early fifties, increasingly competent and sure of herself. When the mother remembers these qualities, her feelings of rejection toward her daughter lessen.

Envy and Competitiveness

Envy, a longing for something the other has, is a common feeling that emerges at times in mother-daughter relationships, causing tension and complicating closeness. We spoke with a woman who feels envious when her daughter talks about her varied and fascinating experiences as a physician. She had once dreamed of having a career like her daughter's, but her parents sent her brother through college and medical school instead of her, and she's never forgiven them. The feeling of envy gnaws away at her, making her feel irritable toward her daughter, even though she doesn't want to be, and reminding her of how limited her life has been.

It's not uncommon for women to envy their daughters' bodies. As Pat tells us, "I try to accept the physical changes and limitations that come with aging, but recently on a walk around the lake with Terri, I was conscious the whole time of her superior strength and endurance. I used to be able to keep up with her, but that day I struggled behind, huffing and puffing, and I had to ask her to slow down several times. It was just a short walk, about half a mile, but every muscle ached afterwards. It's depressing. I try to keep in good condition, but age is catching up with me and I admit I'm envious of Terri's abilities."

Likewise, Pat envies Terri's youthful appearance. She tells us that she used to feel beautiful, but in recent years she's put on over sixty pounds and her body has thickened in all the wrong places. "My face also changed. I had a great complexion when I was young, but the wrinkles have come in droves. People used to think I was a lot younger than I was, and I got a kick out of that, but no more. Now I look at Terri and see a thin, gorgeous, healthy woman in the prime of her life and can't help but feel envious."

Envy can appear at odd moments. One of our interviewees

told us she felt it recently when she became aware that her daughter receives more love and support than she does. The mother's second husband is a decent man but never has made her feel special. When she's with her daughter and son-in-law, however, she observes that their love and appreciation of each other is present in everything they do: the way they speak to each other and with every touch and glance. She has never had a partnership like theirs and can't help but feel envious of her daughter, although she'd never admit this to her.

Mothers often feel uneasy about envy, as though the feeling were shameful and might threaten their relationship. They've absorbed the idea that they should be happy for their daughters' good fortune, rather than covet what they have, and they believe they should express pride in them. When mothers talk to us about envy, they usually put it in this larger context.

"I look at Frida and feel a swell of pride," Cindy tells us. "She's worked so hard to get to where she is, and she's just so successful in everything she does. Sometimes I wonder what it would be like to command all that prestige and respect. I see her breezing along, not having to worry about money, and even though I'm happy for her, I can't help but feel envious."

"Does that feeling affect your relationship?" we ask.

Cindy pauses. "It seems like she's living in another universe, one that is so much easier. I've struggled all my life just to survive, but there she is, living in a beautiful home in Marin County while I live in a shabby rental house on an apple farm. I'm happy for her, sure, but it points out the differences between us, and I feel like a pauper around her."

"Do you wish you had what she has?"

"I really envy her financial security. But I'd never want all that stress or striving for material possessions and professional advancement. I'm poor because I've always believed a person should follow their dream and not get hung up in making money. But don't get me wrong, I'm very happy for her and proud of what she has accomplished. She's an amazing woman."

Feelings of envy sometimes come from daughters as well as mothers. A woman we interviewed, an entrepreneur who started a company that has become internationally successful, says her daughter is envious of her success and suffers because she doubts her own abilities. This gets in the way of their relationship. She yearns for her daughter to confide in her, but that seldom happens because she's too caught up in feelings of comparison and jealousy.

It's hard being the daughter of a successful mother. Florence knows this. As she says, "I try to minimize my professional success when I talk to Rhonda. She's so sensitive, and I don't want to overshadow her. I try to concentrate on what she's accomplishing, even if it's not very much, rather than talking about what I am doing in my life."

Florence also is careful not to say too much about her long, satisfying marriage. "Rhonda doesn't need to hear that from me. She has a hard enough time already with men, and I know she feels like a failure. If I talk about the happiness and good times James and I had while he was alive, it just makes it worse. I don't want to be the object of her envy."

"Rhonda was really close to your husband, wasn't she?"

"Yes, and she was also very competitive about that. She still wants to think he loved her more than Harriet, her brother, or even me. I don't contradict her because she seems to need to feel special in that way."

Another undercurrent in mother-daughter relationships is competitiveness, a strong desire to win or be the best. We hear from one woman that her daughter is deeply invested in being smarter than she is, often correcting her speech and failing to acknowledge how much she knows. The mother feels put down constantly and frustrated by this interaction. She's just about given up trying to have a respectful, back-and-forth conversation.

Mothers, too, have an element of competitiveness in their makeup, although they often don't admit it. We talked at length with a woman in her mid-seventies who is on the downward arc of her career as a research chemist while her daughter is rising to the top of hers in a related field. The mother tells us of the feeling of competitiveness she experienced at a professional conference where her daughter gave a presentation. She remembered her own past successes at public speaking and thought she could do an even better job than her daughter if she were behind the microphone. She immediately felt ashamed of these thoughts, but they resurfaced later in the day when she was repeatedly introduced as her daughter's mother, not as a woman with a professional life and identity of her own. She says she was proud of her daughter but felt competitive because she would have loved to be the one receiving all the praise and applause. She then apologized to us for her feelings, saying she felt embarrassed by them.

Another woman we interviewed has an easier time describing her feelings of competition as she tells us about going away with her daughter for a weekend at a spa in the Catskill Mountains. Each morning they got out of bed early, went to the gym to exercise, and she says she was hyperaware of who could run the longest on the treadmill, who could lift the heaviest weights, who could do the deepest stretches. She wanted to be the best, or at least do these things as well as her daughter, and when she couldn't, she tried all the harder. The problem, she laughs, was that she was so exhausted by all this effort that afterwards she barely managed to float in the Olympic pool while her daughter swam lap after lap.

When we asked if she is competitive with other people, she says no, not with her husband, her friends, or those at the hospital where she still works part time. The feeling seems to emerge only with her daughter, and it has grown in recent years. She wonders if this is because she is defending her place at the top of the pecking order of the women in her family. But, she acknowledges, it's a losing battle because there is no way she can keep up with her daughter as she gets older and less able.

We've heard of mothers and daughters who are competitive with each other around issues of appearance and looks. Which one is dressed the best, which one has the best haircut, which one gets the most compliments? We spoke with a woman who said she and her daughter eye each other all the time, trying to outdo the other. It's sort of a game, but it's also a serious matter. When we ask her why this dynamic exists, she says she thinks it started when her daughter was a teenager and people thought the two of them looked like sisters, and they got in the habit of comparing themselves. When we ask how this affects their relationship, she says they probably would get along better if they weren't so competitive. Maybe, then, they would better appreciate each other.

Many women say they have made their peace with feeling

envious and competitive. They look to their daughters with great pride and are better able to accept the limitations that come with their own aging. As one woman told us, "My daughter is a beautiful, compelling, and flamboyant woman, and I feel like a field mouse beside her. But why should that bother me? She is young and in another stage of life, and our worlds are not the same. Comparing the two of us is like comparing different species."

Many women have told us that their daughters seem to be less envious or competitive with them now than they were when they were younger. As midlife adults, they're well-established in their own lives and no longer threatened by their mothers' successes. They're able to be themselves more fully. This change has healed a subtle tension that existed for years between the two women, and they see each other more clearly now as separate beings.

The Importance of Boundaries

We might argue that boundary violations by mothers or daughters are at the heart of every issue that arises between them. This concept makes sense—it's a fact that tension results if physical, emotional, or psychic space is invaded. But mothers seldom use the language of boundaries to describe their difficulties with their daughters, talking instead about the feelings they have and how they play out in their relationships.

Boundaries are mentioned by mothers only when they talk about daughters who ask too much of them. We interviewed a woman who complained that her forty-two-year-old daughter doesn't take her boundaries into account. She's always needed to be alone first thing in the morning to collect her thoughts and prepare for the day, and while her daughter knows this, she often calls or drops by with requests. Can she leave her sick child with her for an hour while she runs to the grocery store? Who should she get to repaint her kitchen? What should she do about the neighbor who hoards old cars behind his house? The mother is sitting in her old bathrobe, nursing her arthritic joints and trying to enjoy a quiet cup of coffee, and this conversation sets her on edge.

Her boundaries are being ignored, but it's hard for her to be clear with her daughter that this is unacceptable. She's hinted at it, and even asked her daughter to call or come by later in the day, but it will take stronger language to make her understand her needs. She holds back from doing this because she doesn't want to hurt her daughter's feelings or—that old bugaboo—be an unsupportive mother. This situation, with its hesitations, awkwardness, and unexpressed desire, is a common one.

We can't report on the thoughts and feelings of daughters about boundaries because we did not interview them for this book. But we can surmise that they would have a lot to say about how their mothers invade their physical, emotional, or psychic space. Daughters, we posit, are sensitive to boundary violations by their mothers because they had a great deal of power over them while they were growing up, and their presence loomed large in their lives. If daughters experienced their intrusiveness in the past, they are likely to react strongly to it happening in the present day.

But even if mothers have always been careful to be vigilant

about boundaries, they still make mistakes. Perhaps communication is not clear or the wrong assumptions are made, and before they realize it, mothers cross lines and stumble into trouble without warning.

Gloria recounts a time when this happened with Kris. "I arrived at her house while she and her family were gone and noticed that their flower beds were filled with weeds. I figured I'd do them a favor and clean them up before they returned. I found some gloves and a spade in the garage and started in, and after I took care of the weeds, I saw that several bushes had grown wild, and I took out their shears and trimmed a little here, a little there. I was on a roll. But when Kris appeared, she was not at all happy and said I never should have done that without asking her first. She had planned to make the yard a family project that weekend, mobilizing her husband and son, and I had messed up that plan. Also I had trimmed off too much of one of her favorite yellow rose bushes, and she was afraid I had killed it. 'You need to leave my space alone,' she said, very much annoyed. I felt terrible and apologized, and the issue seemed to blow over, but for the rest of the time I was there, I was angry with myself for making that mistake. I'm still astounded by how seriously I misjudged the situation."

Mothers often tell us they have to watch themselves very carefully with their daughters around their boundaries. They try to say and do the right thing as they navigate the anger, rejection, and other feelings that arise between them, but they sometimes fail.

It seems that some mothers and daughters are more graceful than others with boundaries, negotiating them in a more fluid way, intuiting each other's "Do Not Enter" zones with greater ease. Perhaps this is because they are similar in temperament or highly skilled in this kind of interpersonal negotiation, or they understand each other without words. Or they've learned the hard way through the years to respect each other's limitations.

But more typically, mothers bump along, doing the best they can with boundaries, trying to find ways to relate to their daughters without being intrusive or disrespectful. Their attempts sometimes are awkward and mistakes are made, and they fall out of sync for a short or long period of time, then come back together and try again. They learn as they go about what works and what doesn't, and they continue in this way because they cherish these relationships and want them to thrive.

CHAPTER SIX

The Voice Suppressed

~

Mothers yearn to be known and seen by their daughters. They want to share their feelings and thoughts, offer the wisdom they've accumulated, and be recognized for what they've accomplished through the years. However, the melancholy truth is that many of the mothers we've spoken with feel that their daughters know them only in partial ways. They are related to as "Mom" or "Grandma," and even though they are committed to these roles, they feel that their complexity has faded away and their past and present experience ignored.

Mothers and daughters *should* be known by each other—or at least that's what many women think—because they belong to the same families and share a wealth of experience and memories. They remember being strongly connected to their daughters when they were children, yet now they say they sometimes feel like strangers in their presence.

As Margo tells us, "It doesn't seem right. Elise hardly knows who I am, even though I see her almost every day. We've been stuck in the same issues, the same stories, and the same interactions for years."

"Is this because of her depression?" we ask.

"It goes way beyond that. It's something about mothers and daughters," she sadly answers.

When we began our interviews for this book, we didn't expect so many mothers to confide in us that they feel unknown by their daughters. It soon became apparent that this feeling is very much on mothers' minds and worries them. Love and connectedness don't seem to have much to do with whether it exists. Those who are close to their daughters speak about it almost as often as those who are more distant.

When we ask what gets in the way of being more fully known, they say that their daughters don't seem very interested in them, or aren't interested in spending time together, or there's simply too much else going on. But their explanations deepen as they tell us that they themselves contribute to the situation by not fully expressing their thoughts, desires, and memories. Over the years, they have come to hold themselves back so often that the behavior has become automatic.

As Margo says, "How can I expect Elise to know me when I don't tell her much about myself? I'm usually an outspoken person, but something about the two of us keeps my words stuck in my throat."

Margo describes coming home from work that day, feeling frustrated because the furnace in her office building had finally conked out and needed to be replaced. "I saw Elise in the garden as I got out of the car, and I could have told her how upset I was about the broken furnace, and how overwhelmed I felt because I'd have to arrange for a new one, and how sick and tired I am of being the one who has to take care of everything. I could have said it's been like this ever since I was in my teens and my mother got sick, and I feel sad and resentful. It would have felt really good to share these things with Elise—but she doesn't have space for anything more beyond what she's dealing with, so I just said 'Hi' and moved on."

Mothers say that the loss of speech is hurtful to them because they have worked so hard through the years to express themselves and speak authentically in personal relationships, at work, and in their communities. Having witnessed their own mothers censor their language and emotions, they determined early in their mothering that they would break through and create more intimacy with their daughters by being more self-revealing.

Yet so many of them find themselves withholding significant parts of themselves from their daughters at this time in their lives. It's ironic that when they were younger, they learned to speak their minds but now feel daunted in their daughters' presence and carefully measure what they say. Often they don't even have a clear sense of what the wrong words actually would be. Instead they experience a general sense of danger, a fear that leaves them uneasy and hesitant about speaking out.

Fear of Daughters' Anger

Mothers are careful about their speech because they've learned from experience that they might unwittingly say something that will cause their daughters to become angry or withdrawn. Their relationships are so complex and infused with unresolved feelings and unspoken history that they can trip over their best intentions. And because they are so invested in these daughters—often wishing to be even closer to them—they are afraid of this happening.

As a result, mothers who are normally articulate and self-revealing in other areas of their lives watch their speech carefully because of their fear of their daughters' impatience, judgment, disapproval, perhaps even rejection. They become skilled in assessing how much they need to hide of themselves to keep the peace and the connection.

Gloria says that she is careful with both her daughters, but she holds back more with Leanne because of their rocky relationship. "I can't predict what will push her buttons. A while back, in a conversation we were having about feminism, I told her that I had to drop out of college when I got married. In those days wives went to work to put their husbands through college, so that's what I did. I wasn't criticizing her dad, just saying how unhappy I'd been about sacrificing my education, and how this is an example of the sexism that existed then. I thought she'd be interested, but she changed the subject in an angry way. I obviously had touched a nerve, and with anyone else I would have asked what it was—but I was afraid to make her more upset. I won't bring this subject up again."

"Is that a loss for you?" we ask.

"It's frustrating. I'd so much like her to know more about me and my life. I never learned many details about my own mother because she died so young. But I have to cherry-pick what I say, especially to Leanne. Looking back to that conversation about feminism, I can see that I made a mistake by referring to something that happened in my marriage because that makes her feel like she has to defend her dad. But I also can't talk about what happened after the divorce because that reminds her of how hard it was for her then." Gloria pauses. "I'd love to tell her that Judy and I are planning to get married this summer and are very excited about it after all our years together. But she'd probably say something critical, so I'll keep quiet about that, too, until we've actually decided on a wedding date."

"Do you hide important things from Kris, too?"

"It's much easier with her. Her temperament is different, and she's a more forgiving person than her older sister."

"She knows about your wedding?"

"She was one of the first people I told. She loves Judy and is very happy for the two of us, and wants to be my maid of honor. Leanne will probably be at the wedding, but I doubt that she'll enter fully into the spirit and joy of the day."

Fear of Being a Burden

For decades mothers have focused on their daughters' well-being and nurturance, and they're afraid that if they speak too much about themselves and the very real emotional, financial, or health concerns they have, they will upset their finely tuned balance. As a result, they remain quiet about issues important to them.

"I don't want to talk to Terri about my troubles," Pat says. "She doesn't need to hear about them. I'm afraid it would make her feel like she has to take care of me, which has caused problems in the past."

Pat speaks of her fear of being "too much" for her daughter and "leaning too hard" on her. She tries to hide anything that's wrong in her effort to be cheerful. Although she has struggled with depression on and off during her life, she doesn't mention when she's having a bad day. "Some mornings I force a smile on my face and tell myself to cheer up before I stop by Terri's salon. Who wants to see an old, depressed woman dragging through the door? If she asks me how I am, I always say I'm doing great."

"Isn't it hard hiding how you feel?"

"It's better than alarming Terri and having her ask further questions," Pat answers firmly.

Daughters' Lack of Interest

Mothers encourage their daughters to talk about their jobs, relationships, problems, goals, and dreams because they're concerned and interested, and they tend to focus on them in conversations. But all too often, the interest doesn't go in both directions. Their daughters' attention is drawn away, or they're too busy to talk, or mothers sense that they aren't very interesting to them and shortcut what they have to say.

"I know I bore Frida sometimes," Cindy tells us. "If I talk too much, she gets a faraway look in her eyes. Or if we're on the phone, she becomes silent. When that happens, I change the subject and ask her a question about herself. I don't think she even notices what I'm doing."

"How does that make you feel?" we ask.

"Embarrassed and a little hurt. Maybe if I were funnier or more interesting, she would listen. I'm not as quick as she is. When I spend too much time talking about something, she gets impatient and wants me to come to the point." Cindy goes on to say that Frida tunes her out, especially when she talks about her art projects. "I probably give her too many details. I should know by now that she's not interested in hearing about a new way to make paint from wild blackberries, or the pros and cons of framing fabric art."

"Is she interested in how you are?"

"In a general way. But she doesn't want to hear the particulars. I never tell her things she'd find boring, like I was supposed to teach a one-day workshop at a senior center but they called today and said it had to be canceled because there's been a mix-up in scheduling, and now it might not happen until the fall. Things like that."

"Do you talk to her about your feelings?"

"Not very often," Cindy says. "Recently I told her how anxious and frightened I am by my ongoing back pain, and how sometimes at night I lie awake worrying about what will happen if I become incapacitated. She joked that if that's a possibility, I'd better start doing my back exercises. She was right, but that didn't help with my anxiety. I won't mention that again to her. I know she cares about me, but it's on her own terms, in her own fashion, and she doesn't want to hear the hard stuff."

Habits of conversation and routines of attention have been established over the decades, and communication between mothers and daughters is usually quite predictable by the time daughters are middle-aged. Mothers like Cindy know what they can talk about and what should be avoided. They've learned through sometimes painful experience that it's better to err on the side of holding back rather than having their daughters cut them off because they're not interested.

A few intrepid mothers take matters into their own hands,

however, and go ahead with what they want to say even though they sense their daughters' lack of interest. They plunge right in because they figure it's good for their daughters and their relationships if their conversations are more reciprocal. If their daughters turn away, they still have the satisfaction of knowing they at least tried.

Some mothers feel hurt when they sense their daughters' withdrawal of attention, but others don't take their daughters' lack of interest personally because they remember how busy and preoccupied they were in their own midlife years. Children, jobs, and other involvements filled their days, and they didn't have the will or the time to sit and listen carefully to their own mothers. They describe the uncomfortable shock of recognition as their daughters now respond to them in a distracted way, much as they did in the past with their aging mothers.

Hiding Judgment from Daughters

Mothers may feel judgmental about their daughter's choices or priorities and try not to let those feelings seep into the conversation, fearing that they'll alienate them or disrupt their carefully calibrated relationships if they do.

Florence tells us how this works with Rhonda. "She's gone from one wounded man to the next, always feeling that her love will heal them. It hurts me to listen to her romanticized description of each new guy, and sometimes I want to shake her, but I know she's working out whatever she needs to about men. I have to confess I feel judgmental as well as protective. But whatever my complicated feelings are, I keep them to myself."

Mothers talk about their unhappiness with some of their daughters' childrearing practices. While they understand that every generation has to figure out how to mother anew, they see their daughters acting in ways that might cause harm to their grandkids, and they worry about this. They'd like to say something but feel they can't without risking unpleasant fall-out, so they silence themselves.

Florence has a large extended family and is familiar with this dilemma. "My sister complains that her daughter over-structures her grandkids. First school, then afterschool pro-grams, music lessons, sports, play dates, homework. Those kids walk around tense and exhausted all the time. Every moment has to carry the seeds of a learning opportunity, and they never have a chance to go out to play. You know, just for the pleasure of playing. But my sister says she can't and won't talk to her daughter about her concerns because she knows she won't ever accept her point of view."

Florence goes on to describe another relative in her ex-tended family, a cousin her own age who is very concerned because her preteen granddaughter is growing up in a crowded urban neighborhood with limited resources. "I know she wor-ries all the time because her granddaughter has too much free time on her hands and can get into all kinds of trouble. The pull of the street is very strong, and it takes a lot to push against it. The child needs adult supervision after school, a place to be and a time to be there. When my cousin thinks of telling her daughter that she should provide more extensive care for her granddaughter, she holds back. Her daughter is already working two jobs, trying to get ahead, and she'll hear her mother's words as saying she's failing. My cousin just keeps quiet, but she gets over to her daughter's apartment as often as she can to check on her granddaughter and cook her a good meal."

We found it striking that mothers' sense of disapproval or judgment often masks deeper fears for their daughter or grandchildren that they don't feel they can express. It's as though the life experiences they've accumulated and the perspectives they have must be left entirely out of the equation. Mothers chafe to offer their knowledge to ease their daughters' way, but their thoughts are not welcomed. Unless their daughters ask, which they rarely do.

Even though mothers try to avoid talking about their disapproval and judgment, their daughters are often able to "read" them nonverbally. Florence tells us that Harriet and Rhonda joke about the scowl that sometimes appears on her face when she doesn't like what they're doing. "They say I can't fool them," she laughs. "But they're wrong on that. When Harriet came to visit last summer, she started seeing an old boyfriend who had been in trouble recently. Mind you, this is my successful daughter. I thought she was making a big mistake, but I didn't say anything, and she didn't notice my disapproval. If I had gotten on her case, that would have made matters worse, so I kept my face as neutral as I could. I had to trust her good sense, and it turned out that the rekindled romance quickly sputtered out."

Silence Rooted in Shame

Some mothers identify their silence as being rooted in shame about choices they made in the past that have continued to reverberate through the years. Dolores is one of these women.

"I know I messed up big time," she says. "I just wasn't there for my daughter. It was so much easier to turn her over to my mother than to take care of her myself."

When Dolores talks about Yolanda's earliest years, she becomes pensive. "I should have handled things differently. I don't blame her for feeling abandoned by me. Even though I had the best of intentions, I was gone all the time. I worked all hours to support us, and after my divorce I careened from one man to another. My family thought I was wild, and they were right. I was just so young and immature. I'm ashamed that I wasn't responsible then, and I'm ashamed about leaving Yolanda behind when I moved to Oakland, and I'm ashamed about how things went between us when she lived here with me. I didn't do much right as a mother."

"Have you ever spoken with Yolanda about this?"

"And say what? That I'm sorry I was such a failure?" Dolores asks. "That time is past. I am who I am, and the consequences are clear. Yolanda is distant and distrustful. I deserve that. When we talk, I try not to say anything about the past."

Mothers like Dolores avoid bringing up difficult things from the past in order to protect themselves from their daughters' judgment. But as they age and their circumstances change, this withholding becomes increasingly problematic because it creates even more of a gap between them.

We interviewed a recently retired woman who regrets that she didn't save more money in the past for emergencies. Her car has been in the shop for the past month, needing serious repairs, but she doesn't have the funds, and she hasn't told her daughter about this yet. Her neighbors have taken her where she needs to go, but the arrangement can't go on indefinitely.

The mother dreads telling her daughter, her only child, about this situation, and she is trying to gather up the strength to make the phone call.

Fear of Opening Old Wounds

The past continues to haunt and inform the present, leaving mothers hesitant to open old wounds even in the service of cleansing them. For some, it was a divorce that left lasting injury on the psyches of the children; for others it was the mother's exploration of her sexuality at a time before her daughter's own sexuality was formed. Sometimes it was simply failing to give her child the quality of attention she needed. When these issues have never been resolved—as is often the case—many mothers choose to avoid them.

As Margo says, "There are so many landmines. Elise and I get along better if we stay in the present. I never refer to the years when she was young because it's just too painful. She was healthy back then, outgoing and happy, and she doesn't want to hear about that now."

Yet the past exists, and when whole chunks of experience are off the table, it brings an uncertainty into the relationship, leaving mothers scrambling to find their way forward around the painful memories.

"It makes me sad to think how much Elise has changed since she was little." Margo lowers her voice. "I first noticed her becoming depressed after Ted and I almost split up."

"When was that?" we ask, surprised. This is the first we've heard of this.

"She was eleven," Margo says. "I'm not proud of that time. The people in our circles were experimenting with open marriage and psychedelic drugs, and we got caught up in all that. One night Elise wandered into the den and saw my husband kissing another woman. She ran into the kitchen looking for me, but I was sitting in a man's lap, high on drugs and unable to focus on what she was saying. I tried to comfort her, but my pitiful efforts made everything worse. Witnessing all that was terribly traumatic for her, but it got even worse. Ted and I were jealous of each other's flirtations and affairs, and fought all the time. We started to move seriously toward divorce and even separated for three months, but we managed to work our way out of that with a lot of therapy. It's clear that Elise was terribly wounded by all those goings-on."

"And you don't talk about that with her?"

"I've tried, but it's just too painful for both of us, and she deflects every attempt I make. I realize I really let her down. During those years I was self-centered and caught up in my own dramas, and not considering her as I should have. That's hard to admit. She was in the process of developing a sexual self, and there was her mother being sexual all over the place. It must have been awful for her."

Tears spring to Margo's eyes, and she wipes them quickly away. "That part of the past is still hanging there," she says. "You'd think we would have worked it through, but the reality is that not all painful aspects of the past can be resolved with words. Some wounds are lasting. So when I speak with her, I avoid bringing up that time of her life."

Fear of Overshadowing Daughters

~∽~

The mothers we interviewed came to maturity during the second wave of feminism in the 1960s and 1970s, a time when large numbers of women began to insist upon developing themselves both professionally and creatively. Many have achieved success in their work lives, which is greatly satisfying to them, but they tell us they minimize their achievements with their daughters, sensing that their accomplishments can intimidate them and make it harder for them to feel good about themselves.

Florence has learned a lot about how to navigate this in past years. As she says, "It used to be more of an issue with Harriet before she established herself. I held back on telling her about every success I had because I didn't want to discourage her. But since she took this high-profile job, the dynamic has changed and she knows all about my professional life. She and I now are on an adult seesaw. I don't want to get higher up in prestige than she is, but if she gets higher than me that's okay."

"What about Rhonda?" we ask.

"She doesn't like to hear about my successes. They make her feel like a failure. Recently she was at my house when someone from a national newspaper called to interview me about the accomplishments of the Black Lives Matter movement, and she left unceremoniously during the phone call. I knew I wouldn't see or hear from her for several days because she'd need to recuperate."

When we ask Florence if this bothers her, she tells us that she is fully gratified by the acknowledgment she has received from her peers and assures us that she does not need to share this part of her life with Rhonda. "I don't want or need her acclaim," she says.

But not every mother has the same reaction. One respondent told us that she's hurt that her daughter doesn't want to hear about her success, especially because she knows better than anyone else what was involved in getting to this point. The mother believes that her reaction comes from feeling abandoned as a child, and as a result, she tries to be just "Mom" when she's with her daughter, totally focused on her and her life. She's hoping this will repair the past and help her daughter feel her devotion and love. However, as she says, there is much more to her than being a mother, and it pains her that those other parts must be kept hidden from her daughter.

Most mothers are aware of the challenges their daughters face in finding satisfying work in the twenty-first century and sympathize with their difficulties. They understand that the job market is now much more difficult for women over fifty, and they see their daughters unable to turn their skills or training into secure jobs or careers. The last thing they want is to make them feel worse. When they are with them, they sometimes downplay or fail to mention their own successes because they don't want their daughters to become demoralized. Their protective empathy becomes another root of their own self-silencing.

When Life Trajectories Change

We have spoken with mothers who have made sharp turns in the trajectories of their lives, leaving their daughters feeling puzzled and separated from them. These moms often are careful when they speak about their new lives because they don't want to highlight the changes that have taken place or cause their daughters to feel rejected.

We interviewed a woman who immersed herself in a Buddhist practice three decades ago. As she says, "My daughters were just leaving home then. At first they seemed bewildered, but then they simply stopped asking me anything about it. A profound dimension of who I am is unknown to them. My Buddhist practice is the center of my life, especially now that I'm older, but my daughters don't express interest or curiosity. I don't insist on talking about it, and follow the cues they give me. As one of them recently said, 'As long as you're happy, Mom, it's all to the good.' I think that made me sadder than anything she could have said because it felt so dismissive and a little condescending. But I let her remark go."

Conversely we have heard from mothers about daughters who have chosen life trajectories unfamiliar to them. Gloria is one of these. "Leanne has always been clear that she didn't want children," she tells us. "It was probably a wise decision for her, but she will never fully understand who I am because she hasn't had the experience of loving a child. She won't ever go through the things I did as a mom. If she had kids, there's so much I could tell her about myself and my own experience, and she would know me more deeply."

Life keeps changing—and when there is a major change, it can unsettle the mother-daughter relationship. Mothers say they need to be careful on their part to keep the course steady.

Cindy is thinking a lot about that these days because she is moving into a new romantic relationship. "I've been single since my second marriage," she tells us. "I've had various affairs but nothing serious. About a year ago, I met a wonderful woman, and we've been spending most nights together. It's the most satisfying love relationship I've ever had, just what I've been looking for all these years. We're talking about living together, and maybe in the future we'll move to Mexico."

As Cindy describes this unexpected new relationship, her face brightens, but then it clouds over. "I don't know how Frida will feel about this and I'm worried. I haven't said anything to her yet, but at some point I need to tell her. In this day and age, it shouldn't bother her that I'm in a lesbian relationship, but maybe I'm wrong. She's used to me being with men or being alone, and this is a big change. It's just so tricky."

"How do you imagine handling this?"

"My woman friend suggests that she meet Frida in a casual way before I come out to her. That makes sense to me. But I don't know how I will get the two of them together with Frida's frenetic schedule. It's not like we can just drop by her house unannounced and say 'Hey, guess what?' And what if Frida doesn't like her? My friends tell me to relax, it will all work out. I hope it will. I don't know what will happen if it doesn't."

Keeping a Perspective

Everyone has secrets, and mothers often choose not to share important ones with their daughters. Their silence is self-protective and purposeful.

Pat confides that she had a lover, the owner of the construction company where she worked, for several years after she was divorced. "If he had been free, I probably would have married him, but he was committed to his children and didn't want to leave his wife. I respected that. We had something special together that was an addition to both our lives and we saw each other after work whenever we could. Terri didn't need to know about it then, and she doesn't need to know about it now."

Other mothers talk about their sense of loyalty to the secrets of significant people in their families. A recent widow tells us that her husband had been badly beaten as a child, especially around his genitals, and as a consequence, had hardly been sexually active. They had a daughter, but most of the time through their long, satisfying marriage, they were best friends and roommates. As the woman says, her daughter doesn't need to know that history, especially now that he's no longer alive. It was their own secret.

Although mothers often wish they could be more forthcoming with their daughters, they are clear that not everything needs to be said. Details about their intimate relationships, past and present, are and should be off limits, they tell us. Just as they respect that their daughters most decidedly don't want to share details about their sex lives or other relationships with them. Creating and maintaining these appropriate boundaries is important to them.

Mothers keep secrets, but there is still a lot they wish they could share, such as their thoughts about their aging bodies, their experiences of retiring, and their ruminations about how to fill these remaining years. And the more quotidian: the books, the films and TV programs, the exercises they're doing, their various projects and concerns, and the realities that make up their lives.

"I sometimes imagine how satisfying it would be if I could talk more freely with Yolanda," Dolores says. "I would tell her that I painted the bathroom sunset gold last weekend and it looks so much better, and that Vince and I are planning a trip up to Oregon in a camper he's buying. I imagine her knowing me in every way possible. But that's just a dream; it's not at all realistic." She adds that Yolanda has not met Vince yet and knows hardly anything about him, even though the two of them have been together seven years.

Mothers talk about the pain of feeling unknown by their daughters, but in truth, nobody fully knows another person, no matter how close they are to each other. Humans are exceedingly complex, and parts of us are hidden even to ourselves. What people reveal depends largely on their level of trust and the conscious and unconscious parameters of the relationship. The knowledge of another person is always partial. It would be simplistic to think otherwise.

Our mothers understand this, at least in theory. They have had decades of experience navigating relationships with significant others and realize that each one is based on partial rather than complete revelation. Still, they express the desire to be seen in their fullness by their daughters.

An incongruity exists between what they understand is possible and what they want. When we point that out, they tell us that their desire comes at least to some extent from their high expectations. They assume that mothers and daughters should be known deeply by each other because they share the same gender, family line, and cultural context. Husbands, partners, sons, other family members, friends, colleagues all exist—but mothers and daughters are more "the same," or so it seems. Shouldn't that lead to greater intimacy?

Mothers continue to embrace the cultural value of openness that guided them when their daughters were younger. They think that being able to speak frankly to one another is a necessary key to a successful connection and to being seen and known. Even though they find themselves carefully monitoring what they say for very good reasons, they wish they could be more open and transparent with their daughters about who they are and the ongoing issues that shape their aging.

They are aware, too, that the years ahead are limited. At some point in the not-too-distant future, they will no longer be alive to tell their daughters about themselves and their history. They will become a memory, too easily forgotten. If they don't share the details about their life experience while they're alive, they—and their lives—will be lost.

Most of the women we speak with feel unsettled in one way or another about the constraints on their visibility with their daughters. Their yearning is to be spontaneous, free, and *themselves* with them. But there are some who understand that this is not realistic, given the complexities of the mother-daughter relationship, and they begin to recognize that knowledge of each other does not necessarily depend on the exchange of words or information.

Gloria knows this, at least with Kris. "Earlier on I used to ply her with questions about how she was and how she felt, and tried to let her know what was in my mind and heart. But this was too much communication—for her and for me, too. I lightened up, and now I trust that we love each other and are deeply connected, even though we don't talk about everything. This seems to work much better for us."

Daughters need privacy, and mothers can easily feel intrusive to them. But mothers, too, need privacy—and once they let go of the idea that they and their daughters should be "known" by each other in a way that is more extensive than they have with anyone else, they are more able to relax and appreciate what can emerge.

Gloria continues, "I don't see Kris very often, and sometimes our time together seems so fleeting. But recently we took a walk around her neighborhood, and the subject of regrets came up. She said she was sorry about some decisions she'd made in recent years, and we talked about how that felt to her without going into the details. I told her that I'm having more regrets as I'm aging; I didn't name them, just talked about how they're in my mind. We asked each other what we do with these regrets. There were no answers—but it felt like we were knowing each other in a new, really important way."

In the end, the question of voice is one of the most difficult challenges mothers face in their relationships with their daughters. Some women become frustrated, angry, or discouraged by their inability to fully express themselves. They say the time is approaching when they will not be as healthy or as articulate as they are now, and they want to speak before it is too late. Others, though, are more accepting and philosophical. They understand that love is not dependent on words exchanged, and knowledge of one another can and does emerge in a multitude of ways.

CHAPTER SEVEN

The Years Ahead

⟨～⟩

Mothers worry about being a burden to their daughters as they age. They can't help but be aware that they are facing physical and possible mental decline ahead, even if they are now healthy and active. The signs are there: knees or hips may need replacement, winter colds more easily become bronchitis or pneumonia, hearing is less acute, words and names slip away, and many have had cancer or other serious illnesses.

As they consider the future and the decisions that must be made, they're concerned that their need for care and support may demand too much of their daughters and adversely affect their relationships. Already they are aware that their roles with them are changing. No longer are they seen as the stronger, more able ones, and they sense their influence is beginning to fade.

Their daughters are beginning to take charge more often. "When she sees me getting ready to lift something or carry out the recycling, she always steps forward to do it for me," one mother tells us. "I feel warring impulses within myself each time—I want to snatch back the task to show her I can still do it, but at the same time I want to step aside gracefully, accepting her support. I usually go with the second impulse but not without feeling the indignity of growing old."

Mothers talk about approaching a time when they'll need to let their daughters help them more often—but along with this comes a feeling of vulnerability. Many express the fear that their aging bodies may be repulsive, and they worry about smelling or looking "old." We interviewed a woman who said that the extensive varicosities on her legs and thighs have protruded and become knotty in recent years and her daughter was greatly shocked when she saw this. Her mother observed her alarm and quickly covered herself, embarrassed. The shame that aging mothers experience about their bodies can make them feel more vulnerable and afraid of being dependent on their daughters for intimate care in the future.

Mothers are also concerned about greater cognitive slippage and worry that it will affect how their daughters feel about them. One woman told us that she hates the idea of her daughter seeing her make mistakes in what she recalls. "She doesn't yet, as far as I know," she says, "but I'm not as sharp as I once was. The other day she roped me into playing Trivial Pursuit with her family, and I was terrified I'd fail. My memory about those kinds of things is dropping away. I made it through the game, barely, but I'll never, ever do that again."

Subtle changes are taking place and even now, when women can anticipate longer lives, aging is inevitable. At some point decisions about money, housing, and future care need to be made. Many of the mothers we've interviewed have not managed to begin this process, however, and even fewer have communicated their thoughts to their daughters. The daunting task of making all these decisions hangs over them, and they are reminded of it by ads, articles, interviews in the media, and conversations with friends and relatives.

Mothers find it painful and difficult to think about the time ahead. This new life stage requires a different mindset than they've had before, one of thinking about closing down their lives rather than building them up. They feel confused and unprepared for the number of arrangements that must be made and overwhelmed by the feeling of loss. No wonder they often procrastinate.

Daughters, too, help them avoid planning for the years ahead. A mother we spoke with had a mini-stroke last year, and although she recuperated quickly, she is aware that she might have others that would lead to her decline. She understands she needs to get her affairs in order—but her daughter doesn't want to hear about it. Every time she mentions something about becoming less able and needing to make plans, her daughter tells her not to worry, she's fine, and will live a lot longer. The daughter's denial of her health problems and her aging serves as an obstacle in her efforts to make arrangements.

This woman is also held back by the obvious fact that she doesn't know how much time is left ahead. Will she have a massive stroke in the near future or be alive for another twenty or so years? Will she need extensive nursing care, with years of serious decline, or will she collapse and die without warning? She wonders how it's possible to make decisions for the future when everything is so uncertain. If she comes up with a plan, it's likely that an entirely different scenario will unfold and her efforts will be in vain. The alternative—making plans for every future contingency—is beyond her reach. Still, she feels the pressure to move ahead, and she does this in her own way, in her own time.

Most mothers, like this woman, take many years to make decisions for the future and communicate their desires to their daughters. Typically they dip into one issue or another, talking with friends, husbands, or partners, or seeing an attorney, or consulting with their doctor, and they might mention something about this to their daughters. But the process is piecemeal, with stops and starts and reversals along the way, even for those mothers who are ready to face their mortality.

Dollars and Sense

Mothers often begin the process of decision-making for the future with the question of how they are going to support themselves while they're still alive. Money, and how to budget it, is something they've dealt with through the years, and even if they feel anxious about how much they have, it is easier for many to think about this than nursing care, decline, and death.

A few fortunate women have enough income to live comfortably for the rest of their lives. As Margo tells us, "I'm a worrier about money since my parents struggled so hard to support us, but Ted was successful in the real estate market and inherited property from his parents, and I've saved through the years. We have many issues, but thankfully money isn't one of them."

Margo is unusual among the mothers we interview. The majority are single and living on social security and some form of pension, and money is tight. Others are partnered or continuing to work part time, which helps to supplement their income. But even so, most mothers feel financially insecure when they think of the years ahead. Even if they are careful about what they spend, they fear they will have to impose on others—and most likely a daughter—to care for them. The thought of this makes them feel uneasy and ashamed.

Will inflation diminish the value of their savings and pensions? Will the real estate they own or other investments hold up? Will there be a sudden, calamitous need they can't cover? The questions plague them, leaving them feeling vulnerable. The days of finding a new or second job to meet expenses are past, and many can't imagine how they'll survive for the rest of their lives.

Dolores says she can support herself in the future as long as she continues to manage the apartment building. "But that's not going to last forever," she says. "I have macular degeneration, and I'm starting to have trouble reading. When Vince is around, he helps me with bills, contracts, and rental agreements, but he works in Fresno and is here only on weekends." When we ask Dolores what she'll do if she loses her job at the apartment building, she shrugs. "I can't answer that."

Cindy is in an even more precarious position than Dolores. "I have nothing to fall back on," she tells us. "I don't have a pension, and although I get social security, it's not much. It was my choice to lead an artist's life, and I'm certainly not sorry about that, but now I'm paying for it." Cindy goes on to say that she survives by teaching art classes, giving private lessons, and occasionally selling her work. She also gets a cut in rent by watching over the apple orchard where she lives when the landowner, her friend, is away. Sometimes Frida gives her a check for her birthday or Christmas, although she never asks for money. "If I move to Mexico with my woman friend, I'll get by a lot easier because everything is cheaper there," she tells us. "I'm hoping that will work out."

Just about every mother we interview says she doesn't want to depend on her daughter for financial support. Pat, who lives on social security and a pension from her bookkeeping job, feels very strongly about this. "My income doesn't entirely cover my expenses, but fortunately I have a reverse mortgage and that helps. I bought this condo thirty years ago, and I can withdraw a little cash from that mortgage each month. But there's a limit to what I can take out, and I'm scared I'll live longer than the money lasts. I'd never ask Terri to help me. The last thing I want is to be dependent on her. Besides, she has less money than I have because of all her business expenses."

The only mother who would consider asking her daughter for support in the future is Cindy. "If I don't move to Mexico, I'll have to depend on Frida because I'd end up on the streets otherwise. It's getting harder to sell my art and find teaching gigs, and I can barely meet my expenses now. But I'd have to prepare myself to listen to her lecture me about how irresponsible I've been and how I should have saved through the years. And she's right; I have to admit it. I never planned for old age."

"Have you spoken to Frida about this?"

"Not yet. But I'm sure she's figured it out. Every so often she asks me how I'm doing financially, and I tell her."

Passing on Property

Mothers realize early in the process of making arrangements for the years ahead that they need to think about making wills. As Florence says, "When James died, his share of the house and everything else we owned together came to me. We set it up that way. But now I have to rewrite my will, and that raises a lot of questions. There's the house and all our possessions, plus some money tucked away in mutual funds and stock we bought through the years. Should I divide this equally between my kids, or give Rhonda more of it because she has less income and she's less secure? How do I include my grandkids, the rest of the family, and all the organizations I care about?"

Florence is most concerned about avoiding dissention among her grown children. "Harriet's very competent with money, and I've considered making her the executor of the will. I checked it out already with my son, and he's fine with that, but I haven't said anything yet to Rhonda. I can just hear her complaining that her sister is always chosen over her. I suppose I could put her in charge of dispensing my clothing and personal things, but she'd probably sabotage that in some way." Florence pauses. "Maybe I should just turn the whole thing over to my nephew who's a lawyer and let him be the executor. That way, my kids can get mad at him and not each other."

Whatever Florence decides about her will, she knows that her children will think it represents the truth about who she loved most during her lifetime. "I'm veering toward splitting what's there equally between the three of them so nobody's feelings are hurt," she says. "In the meanwhile, I'm starting to pass things on to them that I want them to have. When Harriet was here last time, I gave her my mother's brooch and a string of pearls, and Rhonda now has the gold ring her father always wore. My son and his wife entertain more than I do, so I passed on my silverware to them. I'll continue giving away these heirlooms so that there won't be any fights about who gets what after I die. I've seen how families can split apart with that kind of bickering."

We spoke to some mothers who have decided not to pass on money to their daughters. "Whatever I have—and it won't be much—will go to Judy," Gloria says. "I've lived with her all these years in the house she owns, and she's been there for me in a million ways. She deserves it."

"Have you talked to your daughters about this?" we ask.

"They both know. Leanne certainly doesn't need anything from me, and I've helped Kris financially through the years when she's been in trouble. They agree that it's fair that my partner gets whatever money there is."

"No hurt feelings?"

"Kris said she wants my jewelry and the photos from her childhood, and I told her of course, that's fine." Gloria pauses. "I'm fortunate my daughters are easy about this. I recently talked to a friend whose two daughters have been fighting about their inheritance for the last ten years. It started when my friend wasn't even sixty and in perfect health. One daughter was demanding that she get her mother's house after she died and the other said no, it should go to her. The quarrel went back and forth until my friend stopped it recently by saying she's decided to sell the house now and move into a senior facility. The daughters were furious, but the fight con-

tinues about who gets everything else. How disgusting is that?"
Some mothers do not bother making wills. "It's unneces-
sary," Cindy says. "I don't own anything, and if I did, it would
automatically go to Frida as my only descendent."

"What about your studio supplies and your personal things?"

"She'll get those, although she'll probably hire someone to
haul them right away. But I've made a special packet for her
that she'll find in my desk drawer once I'm gone." Cindy's eyes
brighten. "I hope it will mean something to her. I've put together all the photographs I have of her from the past, and I've
written her a long letter. I spent hours pouring out my heart,
telling her how much I loved her even if I failed as a mother,
and I wrote about my values and what's been important to me.
It's sort of like an ethical will. I reminded her that there are
more important things than money and accomplishments, and
she should take the time to enjoy the beauty of the earth and
all of creation. And then I ended it by giving her my blessing
for a good life."

"That sounds beautiful," we say, touched.

"I just hope reading the letter has the same meaning for her
that writing it did for me."

When daughters are thriving and self-sufficient, mothers
don't need to worry about leaving them money to ensure their
future survival. But those with troubled daughters face a par-
ticular dilemma. "What is going to happen to Elise when I'm
gone?" Margo asks. "She is so vulnerable. She can hardly get
herself out of the cottage to buy groceries, much less hold a job
to provide for herself and her son."

"She'd inherit money from you, right?"

"There'll be a monthly allowance from a fund the bank will

manage. I'd never trust her with more than that. But money is just the most obvious concern. I can't imagine Elise being in the world without me watching over her." Margo sighs. "I lie awake at night worrying about this. But I tell myself she's better off than a lot of other physically or mentally disabled daughters. At least she won't be out there on the streets, trying to survive. I'm so glad there are enough resources in our family to provide for her. I've known plenty of women who are taking care of their ill, dependent daughters, and when they die, there is no safety net for them. That's really heartbreaking."

Preparing for Decline

Almost all mothers say they want to stay in their own homes for the rest of their lives. Their hope is to be independent and self-sufficient, declining gracefully in comfortable, familiar surroundings and dying in their own beds, surrounded by those they love.

This is the dream but not always the reality.

Living at home can become logistically difficult or impossible after a serious accident or illness. The bedroom on the second floor is suddenly out of reach and a hospital bed or cot must be moved into the living room. Bed baths and nursing care become a part of the daily routine, and cooking and cleaning, which used to be so easy, are now out of the question. The garden outside, once the greatest pleasure, is quickly becoming overgrown.

Or the mind no longer can hold the difference between day and night. The task of bathing and dressing is forgotten; the gas on the stove is turned on, but where is the pan and what should be cooked? People's names float beyond reach, although the death of a beloved puppy sixty years ago still brings tears to the eyes.

Mothers approach the years ahead with a feeling of dread. They've heard stories about old women who are disheveled and wandering about, or ill and unable to keep up their homes, and they push away the fear that this will be their future. They resolutely move forward, clinging to the lives they have so carefully crafted. They keep in mind visions of women who thrive to the end of their lives, gardening, visiting with friends, taking classes, and volunteering, and they hope they will be lucky enough to spend their final years this way.

But what are their chances of this happening? "Both my grandmother and mother had horrendous ends," Pat says. "One became seriously paranoid and had to be hospitalized, and the other had bone cancer that metastasized and was terribly painful. I'm scared that something like that will happen to me."

Pat has diabetes and hypertension but does everything she can to stay in shape by going to yoga classes, watching her diet, and trying to walk regularly, although it's harder now than it used to be. "As of now, I'm more or less okay," she says. "A little depression, but I can still take care of myself."

A housekeeper comes to her condo weekly to do the heavy work, and even though Pat regrets the cost, she's glad to have that support. "But I know what's coming," she says. "Two years ago I had hip surgery and a long recuperation. Terri, bless her, wasn't much help, but her partner stopped by twice a day to see how I was doing and drove me to physical therapy. My friends from the church also brought over casseroles, so I made it through."

"Were you disappointed that Terri didn't come through for you then?" we ask.

"I've become used to her being like that. But it was a reminder that I can't count on her in the future. She always withdraws or gets irritated if I'm needy, even if it's a physical problem. And now that her partner isn't in the picture anymore, I don't have anyone in the family who would take over."

"What will you do?"

"Thankfully I have long-term health insurance that would help cover the cost of nursing care if I need it. That gives me a shot at staying in this condo rather than moving into assisted living or another place. I'm scared to death of ending up in some kind of depressing facility."

Pat is privileged because of her long-term health insurance. Many mothers don't have this resource, and they face huge bills if they need nursing care in their own homes. "A woman who lives in this condo complex has a degenerative nerve disease that will probably kill her in the next few years," Pat says. "She has to sell her condo and move to a nursing facility because her expenses have already eaten up her savings. It's tragic. Even though her daughter loves her and flies in as often as she can, she lives in Atlanta and can't put everything aside to take care of her."

Mothers often review who would be around to help if they need care. "I can't lean on my children," Florence says. "Harriet would come if there's a crisis, but she can't stay. My son and his wife are too busy, and Rhonda isn't reliable. But I have a lot of relatives around here who would make sure I'm taken care of—my sister and two nieces, to begin with, and the folks at my church." A worried look crosses her face. "Eight years ago I was diagnosed with lymphoma. I'm in remission, but realistically, the cancer could return at any time. That makes planning for the future all the more on my mind."

"Would you consider moving in with Harriet?" we ask.

Florence thinks about this for a moment before answering. "She'd take good care of me and we get along, but no, I wouldn't do that. This is my home, and this is where I belong. It's where James and I spent so many years. I don't want to leave it unless I have to."

Most mothers echo Florence's decision not to move in with their daughters unless there is no other option. They fear either they would be too much of a burden or they'd lose their autonomy. However, we know a few women whose daughters live thousands of miles away, and they already spend part of the year in their homes. Most of them say the arrangement works out well because they can care for themselves and are able to contribute to the household. But if they were to become ill and more dependent on them, they fear it would create too much of a strain.

A few others have told us that they expect to move in with their daughters in the last years of their lives because this is the tradition in their families. "I'll be independent for as long as possible," one mother tells us, "and then I'll go to be with my daughter. My own mother moved in with me at the end, and it was a precious experience, one I'll never forget. In our family we believe that death is a natural part of life, and that includes changing soiled diapers, bathing and feeding, and sitting by the bedside through the night. It's all part of what we do for each other in our family."

Such loving, total care cannot be expected in most families.

Daughters are too busy, or would become resentful or awkward with such intimacy, and mothers would have difficulty accepting it. As a result, many mothers consider moving into retirement communities, elder homes, or nursing facilities to avoid having to rely on them. As Gloria says, "It seems that everyone my age is talking about this possibility, researching which places are best and which to avoid. One of my hiking buddies has found a wonderful facility and is on the waiting list—but I bet she won't go there when she reaches the top of it because she hates being around a lot of people. Some other friends, though, are comfortable with that, and if they had to move there, they'll do it willingly."

"What about you?" we ask.

"I'm in this house until I die," Gloria answers. "I like living in this neighborhood among people of all ages and backgrounds, not just old people. Judy says she'll take care of me for the rest of my life, and here's hoping that works out. But Judy's had a round of breast cancer, so you never know. If she dies before me and I have a serious illness, I'll find a way to cut my life short so that I don't have to move into one of those places." Gloria's plan to avoid going into a nursing facility would be considered extreme or unacceptable by some people, but it reveals how strongly she feels about being pushed there by circumstances.

Daughters and Diminishment

When mothers begin to plan for their remaining years, they typically talk with their partners and friends because they find it easier to discuss these sensitive, difficult matters with those their own age. But daughters, at some point, need to be included in their conversations unless they and their mothers are completely estranged. The decisions that are made will impact their own resources, as they are the ones who most likely will help to implement their mothers' wishes.

Yet daughters are not always receptive to having these conversations. As Pat tells us, "I recently told Terri I was worried about whether I could manage to stay in the condo in the future. She brushed me off by saying there's plenty of time ahead for that conversation. We were having a glass of wine together, enjoying ourselves, and I didn't want to wreck the occasion by pushing her further."

Pat admits that she was at least partly relieved when Terri changed the subject. "Maybe she's right and I will live another fifteen years, so why worry about this now?" she smiles. "Lots of women are active and healthy into their nineties."

"Will you bring all this up again?" we ask.

"I'm not sure," she says. "Terri and I are getting along so well these days, and I don't want that to change. If I talk more about becoming diminished, she'll start to see me in a different light. She'll get scared that I'm becoming needy and she'll have to take care of me, and then she'll pull away. It's happened so many times before."

"It sounds like you need to be upbeat around her all the time. That's a lot of pressure."

Pat sits silently for a moment. "I'd rather suffer that pressure than have her withdraw from me."

Some mothers, like Pat, know that their daughters are uncomfortable with their aging and frightened of the needs that might emerge, and they respond by postponing a discussion about the future. Others have different reasons for putting off this conversation.

"I'm afraid it would make Elise feel even more anxious," Margo tells us. "It's best for me to decide what I want in the future and make the necessary arrangements, and then I can let her know what's going to happen when the time comes. Elise is deeply insecure, and I don't want to remind her of the fact that I'll be gone at some point."

"Even though she knows it?"

"The only hope for her right now is to feel solid and secure. That's why Ted and I support her and let her stay in the cottage." Margo hesitates. "I'm sorry I can't bring her into a conversation about the future, though. It would help me feel less anxious myself—but I know it would be destabilizing for her."

Margo goes on to tell us how her mind begins to spin when she tries to imagine what it would be like if Ted dies before her and she's ill and unable to care for herself. She thinks that planning is important, and she talks often about these issues in her long-standing women's group, which she says is a safe place to reveal her fears. But even though she appreciates the support from the group, she feels she hasn't been very successful yet in figuring out what to do, and she continues to be overwhelmed by all the details. "Maybe it's a good thing I'm not talking with Elise about the future, because I'd just get more confused," she says.

We ask Margo if she knows other mothers who postpone having conversations with their middle-aged daughters about these matters. "My closest friend's daughter is bossy and opinionated, so my friend doesn't want to talk to her yet," she answers. "She's afraid that she will take over planning for her future and pressure her to go along. When my friend had back surgery last year, her daughter moved in and directed her every move. She even told people not to call her or come by, but my friend would have felt a lot better with company. It was like she was in jail, and she finally had to ask her daughter to leave. She knows she needs to include her in planning for the future, but she's not ready. Especially because she's considering selling her house and moving to Hawaii—not what her daughter has in mind—and she knows she will have a fit once she hears."

Most mothers feel very strongly that they don't want to lose their autonomy and independence in the future. They fear being under their daughters' control and not being in charge of themselves. As Dolores says, "I'm an independent cuss. When I was last in San Antonio, Yolanda told me several times that I should stop smoking because it's ruining my health. I have a chronic cough, and I suppose the effects of smoking show in my skin and have something to do with my eye problems. Well, she can criticize me about this, but I'm going to do what I want to do, even if it shortens my life."

Dolores goes on to tell us about a woman friend of hers in her late eighties who is now living with her midlife daughter. "My friend has crippling arthritis pain and can't get out of the house much, and I visit her when I can. We sit around, drink coffee, and have a cigarette together. I asked her if smoking is a problem with her daughter, and she said no, her daughter understands that she doesn't have many pleasures left in life and accepts it. I know if I were living with Yolanda, she'd hide my cigarettes and forbid me to smoke. She'd say she was doing it for my benefit, and also so I wasn't a bad influence on her kids."

"Do you think she's concerned about your welfare?"

"Maybe. A little." Dolores pauses. "But she's also controlling in her own quiet way."

A basic question emerges for mothers with their daughters: how much do they trust them to care for them in a loving, kind, competent way when they need help in the future? Many feel extremely vulnerable or wary about giving over or sharing control with them, and they resist doing this to the end of their lives. Others are more open and allow their daughters entry into planning for the future, and they move with greater ease into growing dependency. Their willingness depends on many factors, among them how trustworthy their daughters have shown themselves to be, how close they are to them, how much help they need, and how comfortable they are with being dependent.

Anticipating Death

The issues of money and future care are on mothers' minds as they age, as is the question of how to handle the end of their lives. Some feel its approach in a more immediate way than others, but everyone knows death is coming, and nobody knows when. The need emerges for them to think about how they want to handle this final experience, what kind of death they want, and what they'd like to have happen with their bodies afterwards. Like other concerns they face in this stage of life, the answers to these questions do not come all at once and typically involve talks with significant others, friends, and doctors, as well as thoughtful consideration and a fair amount of internal struggle.

At a time when mothers are becoming more aware of the passing years, the questions around the end of life perhaps are the most difficult. Dying is the final step in the process of letting go, and it is the hardest, the saddest, and the most challenging to accept. At the time of death, they most likely will be in the hands of those closest to them, their doctors, and possibly hospitals, and will no longer have control over their care.

When mothers begin to think about this, they typically designate a power of attorney to make decisions about their medical care in case they become incapacitated. The process of deciding who to pick is complicated for those who don't have living partners or an obvious first choice for this role. If they have to choose between several children, feelings can be bruised. They wonder how to explain their choices to those they've passed over and how to soften the fact that they trust one child more than the others to carry out their wishes.

"When I decided that Harriet would be my health-care power of attorney, Rhonda didn't like it," Florence says. "She made the case that she lives close by so she should be the one. I told her I saw her point, and I'd put her second on the list in case Harriet wasn't available during an emergency. I knew that this was just one more slap in her face from a mother who has never appreciated her the way she has wished, and I was sorry about that, but I have to take care of myself and do what's most comfortable for me. The last thing I need is a daughter who doesn't show up when I need her or who becomes hysterical on the spot. Harriet is calm and steady, and that's what I want."

Mothers wonder where they will spend their final days. Can daughters or other relatives care for them in their own homes, or will the care come from hospice or nurses in a hospital? Will they die with their loved ones by their side, or surrounded by strangers, or alone? Each woman has her own set of preferences about these things, and as they age, they begin to feel the need to state them to those close to them or in a document.

Dolores tells us that recently she went through a class her health-care providers offered during which she was asked to state her wishes for her end-of-life care. "I'd never thought about some of those things before," she says. "It really shook me up. One of the questions was who did I wish to be with me when I was dying. I realized I wanted a very quiet atmosphere, with Vince there holding my hand and maybe a few other people like his daughter and my neighbor friend in the background."

"What about Yolanda or your other relatives?"

"They'd want to come. My family is like that when people are dying. But there's too much unfinished business between us, and it would make me tense to have them around. I've told Vince to let them know after I've passed, not while it's happening."

Moving Ahead with Daughters

As mothers make decisions about the years ahead, they understand they need to talk with their daughters about their wishes. As we've said, they might resist these conversations at first because they feel vulnerable, or not ready, or don't want to face their inevitable decline and dependence. They are invested in continuing their lives as usual, accommodating as best they can to a decreasing sense of vigor or a fading memory. But the daughters are usually brought in somewhere along the way. Some women make all their decisions first before they approach them. This is Gloria's style. "I knew exactly what I wanted," she says. "Assuming Judy lives longer than I do, I decided she would be in charge, but just in case, I also gave Kris all the details. There's a list of where all my important papers are, and my passwords, medical information, and so forth. Also my desires for cremation, not burial, and where I want my ashes scattered. When I gave the list to her, she seemed rather relieved and thanked me."

"Will you also give the list to Leanne?"

"Probably not. As long as one daughter knows, it's enough. Besides, Leanne would have opinions about everything, and I don't need to struggle with her around that. I want to keep things simple, and I trust that Kris would carry out my wishes without challenging them."

Some mothers confer with their daughters about the arrangements they want as they go through the process of deciding. Florence tells us, "Harriet and I first starting talking about these matters when she was here three years ago. It was before James passed, and she saw what I was dealing with in taking care of him and asked me directly about myself." Florence pauses. "Up to that point I hadn't thought about it much because I was focused on James, but she got me thinking about the decisions I needed to make. We talked a lot about where I wanted to live and if I have the means to hire nursing care if I

need it. I went over my finances with her so there's no surprises."

Other mothers avoid making decisions about the future
because they are overwhelmed and don't even want to think
about it. As a result, the subject isn't mentioned with their
daughters. Cindy confesses, "I can't make up my mind about
any of these things," she says. "I figure it will work out one way
or another. When the time comes, Frida will do what is necessary. She's much smarter than I am in that department."

Those mothers we interviewed mostly are tiptoeing their
way toward the future, concerned about the effects of becoming more dependent on their daughters. They struggle with
feelings of pride and shame and imagine worst-case scenarios
of the disintegration of these relationships. However, the reality
of growing dependence can be less disturbing than they anticipate, as some older mothers are beginning to learn. One woman
who has had a contentious relationship with her daughter
through the years tells us that she is discovering that her
daughter loves her more than she ever realized. "What a pleasure, what a joy," she says. "I see more of her now. She comes to
check up on me often and brings in food and the prescriptions
I need. It's like a great hostility has dropped away. Maybe it's
because she is more in charge, or maybe it's because the issues
of competition and control are no longer alive between us—but
whatever is causing this, I'm the happy recipient."

Margo isn't at this point in her life yet, but she had an experience of greater closeness with her mother in her last years
and thinks about that often. "For a lot of my mom's life she was
like a ghost, existing but not really living because of her depression. But when she was eighty, she was diagnosed with

pancreatic cancer and I came to stay with her to the end. Even though she was in pain, her depression seemed to lift and she talked a lot about her life, how she felt about all of us, what she wished for us. It was just the most precious time for me, a great gift." Margo pauses. "Will it be this way with Elise and me? I can only hope."

CHAPTER EIGHT

A Time of Reckoning

As mothers age, they become thoughtful about their lives, reviewing the pleasures, satisfactions, disappointments, and sorrows they've experienced and considering what they might have said, or done, or even now do differently to change the course of events. It is as though a veil has been lifted, and they're able to see themselves in both the past and the present with greater clarity.

Mothers have much to reflect upon at this time of life. They have buried their parents, lost other family members, friends, and colleagues, and are experiencing the process of decline within their bodies. For most, their full-time work lives have ended, and they are left to find meaning and value in their days. Time is limited, and they feel a growing urgency to repair what has gone wrong in their significant relationships or to speak the words that have not been said. No longer do they have unlimited years ahead in which to sort through the tangled connections that exist.

As they become aware of the fragility of their lives, they focus on a narrower group of family and friends. They become much more focused on intimacy and being connected to loved ones, and they are drawn to those things that make them feel purposeful in the world.

Mothers know that their primary relationships are not set in stone and continue to change, which requires flexibility and awareness of the subtle currents that run under the surface. As one woman told us, "It isn't over until it's over." She and her daughter had a long history of being critical toward each other, but recently there was an unexpected opening. "I really can't explain it," she said. "It's as though something softened in both of us. We were boarding a ferry to San Francisco, and I tripped and hit my head on a metal ledge. Fortunately I wasn't injured, but it shook me up, and the ferry captain had me lie down for a while. My daughter stood over me, her eyes worried and full of love. I recognized how concerned and protective she was, something I had never seen or at least allowed myself to acknowledge. I reached for her hand and said, 'I love you, too.' We never talked about that moment afterward, but our relationship has softened and eased in so many ways, and I'm grateful."

A great range exists in how mothers navigate this time of facing their limitations and errors in judgment. Many have already begun the process—with regret and sorrow, and an acknowledgment that though they might do things differently had they another chance, they accept why they made the choices they did. Others feel overwhelmed by all their memories and feelings, and are far from accepting or making peace with the outcome of their earlier choices. Coming to terms with one's mistakes, poor judgment, and misplaced priorities takes a certain kind of fearlessness. As one woman we interviewed said, "Who would think that so much courage is required at this time of life?"

For some, this time of reckoning is intensely painful. "When I was younger," Margo tells us, "I really worried about

Elise's mental health and focused most on how she should take care of herself. But now, I'm much more aware of my part in what has happened to her." She pauses. "The process of self-awareness began when I went to a week-long Buddhist retreat. I imagined I would have a restful break from work, but as I sat on my meditation cushion day after day, I couldn't stop thinking about how terribly I've treated Elise. The truth is that I've always preferred her brother to her, and I saw how rejecting and judgmental I'd been. I no longer could avoid that failure on my part."

Guilt and Shame

Margo has led a privileged life in many ways, yet she suffers from a heavy dose of guilt and shame. "I obsess constantly about what I've done to Elise. When I speak about her with people I know, I generally say it's worrisome to have a depressed daughter, and sometimes I complain a bit about how hard it is for Ted and me. Those are not lies, but they're only a tiny bit of the truth. Underneath I feel like such a complete failure. I've tried so hard to love her, but I just can't seem to do it, or at least do it right. And I'm sure she feels that and hates me for it."

"You're there for her in a lot of ways," we say.

She gives us a sharp look. "Yes, but it's tainted by my negativity toward her. I know firsthand how it feels to be unloved and how that leaves such emptiness and pain. My mother adored my younger brother, and that was clear from our earliest years. He could do no wrong, but she was closed off to me and unloving. I could see her feelings about me in her eyes, hear it in her words. When she became ill and depressed and unable to leave her room, I felt that was the final rejection."

"Yet you survived."

"My *bubbe* loved me. I was fortunate to have her fill in the lonely places." She pauses. "Elise never got that special kind of affirmation. From anyone."

Margo tells us that she never intended or imagined that she would treat her daughter in a hurtful way. "But here I am, a woman in her seventies who has repeated the harm that was visited upon me, loving my son more than I was able to love my daughter. It's a textbook case—and how painfully ironic that I, as a psychologist, didn't catch on to what I was doing until it was too late."

Margo is going around in circles, blaming herself for what has happened with Elise and paralyzed by her sense of failure, and we realize that she's a long way from coming to any sort of resolution about their relationship or acceptance of her part in it. We hope that she finally reaches that point, but it is not guaranteed. Some mothers struggle with shame and guilt to the end of their lives, never forgiving themselves for what they've done or how they've felt, castigating themselves over and over.

"That's very sad," we say to Margo.

"Yes, it is," she answers somberly.

Bound by History

Margo's sense of failure comes from how she has mothered Elise and the negative feelings she continues to have about her.

She blames herself, not her daughter, for what has gone wrong and is far from making peace with their relationship as it now is. We've spoken with other mothers who share the same lack of resolution within themselves but say instead that the disjuncture with their daughters is the result of earlier traumatic or painful events such as battles within the family, violence, or abuse. Whatever the trauma, it continues to hover over the relationship, and mother and daughter cannot find a way to move beyond their past to heal.

Gloria struggles with this as she reviews her life. "My trouble with Leanne started when my husband and I broke up. I don't regret the divorce for one minute, but it was so traumatic for her. There was a lot of fault and responsibility on both of our parts but she doesn't see it that way. She feels that he was the innocent victim and I was the one who caused all the pain and sorrow."

"And now?"

"Her judgment never seems to change. She referred to it again recently when she invited me out for drinks. She was on her third glass of wine, more loose-tongued than usual, and I said that I'd heard that my brother's daughter, her cousin, was getting divorced. She made a nasty dig about how my side of the family can't seem to stay married, and I took the bait and asked what she meant. 'You dumped my dad,' she answered angrily. 'He really didn't deserve that.'"

Gloria shakes her head. "What could I say? Her dad has been telling her the divorce was my fault for the last forty years, and she believes him. There's no way I can defend myself against that. Life has gone on all that time, he's been married to someone else, and Judy and I are happy together—but

Leanne still can't seem to get over it. The tension hangs in the air between us and never goes away."

"Do you think that dynamic will change?"

"And she'll be open to me? Realistically, no. But I'm an optimist, and hope that maybe she'll be a little more forgiving in the future. Although she'll probably never understand me or my life."

"Can you live with that?"

Gloria takes a deep breath. "What's my choice? Judy tells me to let go of my unhappiness and accept that there's nothing I can do to change the way Leanne feels. She's right about that, I know, but I'm not there yet."

When an earlier trauma is still alive, it continues to shape how mother and daughter are able to talk to one another and what's possible between them. As Gloria says, "My relationship with Leanne would have been very different if she weren't still so attached to the wounds of the past. Sometimes I imagine confronting her about this and insisting she give up being so unhappy. Life is too short, and why waste it on grieving over the past? " She stops. "Do I think that would work? No. There's too much water under that bridge."

If Gloria is fortunate, she and Leanne will find their way to a stronger connection in the years ahead. Gloria, at seventy-six, is still healthy, but she will become more vulnerable in the future, and perhaps Leanne will respond with sympathy. Or Leanne might learn somewhere along the way that right and wrong are not absolutes. Or perhaps she'll realize that she has been unfairly blaming her mother for everything that went wrong, and Gloria will be able to forgive her. Or perhaps none of these things will happen, and Leanne will continue to be angry and resentful, and Gloria will continue to suffer from their lack of connection to the end of her life.

Defeat and Resignation

As mothers increasingly look back over the past, some feel defeated by the state of their relationships with their daughters. Unable to change them, they sink into a sense of hopelessness.

Dolores says, "What has happened with Yolanda is bothering me more now. When I was younger, I didn't think about it as much because I was always busy and felt like I had the rest of my life to set things straight. But time is passing by so fast, and who knows how much I have left? My father died in his early seventies, and I could, too."

"Do you hope that things will ever get better with Yolanda?"

"I'm afraid that possibility's over between us. She'll always think of me as the mother who abandoned her."

"What about when her grandmother dies? She won't have that steady presence to rely on anymore," we say. "Maybe there would be an opening for you then?"

"Too much has happened between us," she answers flatly.

By this time we've seen the depth of Dolores's sense of defeat. She might be right that she and Yolanda will always be alienated, but another mother in a similar situation might accept the situation with less pessimism than she does. Or try to reach out to her daughter more often without expecting to change anything. Or begin to move toward forgiving herself and her offspring.

Defeat and resignation can be important steps in the process of coming to terms with relationships that have fallen short of what they might have been. These feelings acknowledge all that has gone wrong and are important in understanding the larger picture. But the danger is that the discouragement mothers experience at this time can stop them from reaching out to their daughters or noticing and responding if there are small, unexpected openings for connection. Not much can change if the story of the relationship has already reached its dismal conclusion in the mother's mind.

Yet there is something to be said for defending against the sorrow of a broken relationship. As Dolores says, "I don't even want to think things between us could be better because that just raises my hopes. It's easier to think of Yolanda as a lost cause. I know that's cynical, but I feel safer this way than looking for the relationship to change."

The Shadow of Disappointment

Almost all the mothers we've interviewed speak at some point about being disappointed in their daughters or in the quality of their connection. As Pat says, "Nobody is perfect, and that includes Terri. If I had my way, there are things about her I'd change. Like her temper and her impatience with me when I'm sick or need her."

Pat acknowledges her regrets and has learned through the years to mask her neediness and vulnerability so that Terri doesn't withdraw. She understands now that this dynamic in their relationship echoes the one she had with her mother. "My mom did that same thing of pulling away from me if I needed her. That was really painful to endure as a child, and I've had to accept it with Terri. I'm especially sensitive to rejection, and always have been. When Terri was born, I imagined she would love me in a way I hadn't been loved before, but I realize now that was totally unrealistic and unfair to her. She couldn't make up for my unhappiness as a child, and it took me a lot of soul searching to understand and accept that I had put pressure on her to do that without realizing."

"And now?"

"I still wish she would come through for me more, but I've grown to be more philosophical about it. I used to feel like a terrible mother for being disappointed in her, but I realize it's just part of the mother-daughter package, a natural feeling that comes and goes like a shadow."

Pat has made peace with her feelings about Terri and doesn't blame herself anymore. But since their relationship has been closer and more satisfying in recent years, it is easier for her to reach this point of acceptance than it is for mothers with more troubled connections.

One mother we interviewed told us she struggles with her daughter's lack of ambition. She describes her as smart and talented, yet she decided not to go to college and has wandered from place to place and job to job. As the decades have passed, the mother's disappointment has intensified. She knows her daughter is aware of her judgment because she seldom comes to visit and rarely responds to her phone calls. The relationship is fractured, and the mother is deeply disappointed about that, too. A double whammy, she calls it.

For this unhappy mother, the sense of disappointment has been the main theme of the relationship rather than a shadow that comes and goes, as it does for Pat. She is belatedly realizing that she has lost her daughter because of her obsession with her lack of stability, and she's weighed down by regret for how she has been and wonders if the two of them can ever regain a sense of connection.

Acceptance

This mother is far from accepting the reality of her relationship with her daughter. Instead she condemns herself for how she has been as a mother and mulls over the past, reliving her mistakes. Many women go through a painful period like this when they are more able to clearly see their own part in the failure of their connection with their daughters and no longer can avoid the consequences of the wounds they have caused.

Some remain in this introspective state for extended periods of time or even until the end of their lives. But the lacerating repetitiveness of so much self-blame is painful, and many move on to a more nuanced understanding and acceptance of their relationships. Florence tells us how this shift emerged for her. "I went through a time before James got so ill when I thought a lot about how I'd been as a mother. It was precipitated by something my sister said when I was talking to her about a problem I was having with Rhonda. She said, 'No wonder that girl is so needy; she didn't get much mothering when she was younger.' I couldn't answer. My sister wasn't being critical, just stating a fact, but I had never put it to myself like that before."

Florence goes on to say that her sister's remark sank in,

and she pondered it for weeks afterwards. "I realized I had been dismissive toward Rhonda. I'd never meant to be, but that's what happened. I hadn't paid much attention or warmed up to her through the years, and I hadn't worried about it because James loved her, and they were so close. Once I recognized my behavior, I felt I'd failed her and didn't know how to move on from there."

But Florence didn't stay defeated for long. "One day I was walking in my neighborhood and saw a garden that had some piles of weeds and shrubs with beautiful roses," she says. "You couldn't say that garden was just weeds or just flowers because it was both. And I thought that's how it is with Rhonda. Our garden is good times and bad times, fighting and making up, loving and not loving, all put together. My failing her as a mother is part of it, too, but it's not the whole thing."

"What happened when you came to this understanding?"

"It calmed me down. And since then I've made more of an effort to listen to her and love her for herself. Sometimes I get impatient and find her difficult, and I'll probably always be that way because I'm not the kind of person who puts up easily with foolishness. But she needs support, especially now that James is gone, and she'll always be my baby."

I Did My Best

Once women acknowledge and accept how they have fallen short of being the perfect mothers they wished they had been, they are on the way to making peace with the past. An important step is being able to say that they did the best they could.

This does not mean wiping away or diminishing how they harmed their daughters or contributed to their relationships' troubles. Instead they recognize that even though they fell short, their intentions were honorable and they didn't intend to cause pain.

Cindy never has had difficulty describing what she's done wrong as a mother with Frida. She's insecure, self-critical, and apologetic about her mistakes, and if she ever forgets them, Frida is only too happy to remind her. But she is slowly beginning to come to terms with this part of her past.

"I used to feel I was a complete disaster as a mother," she says. "But more recently I've realized I did the best I could. I was so young and idealistic, and clueless about how to exist in the world. Coming from my background, I didn't have a model for how to be a mother. I knew I didn't want to be strict and angry like my own mom was, but what did that mean?" Cindy stops and then continues, "I'm not saying I've forgotten my mistakes, but I'm also recognizing some of the things I did were right. I've always truly loved Frida, and even though I dragged her through some very rough times, my heart was in the right place, and it still is."

"Does she know this?"

Cindy smiles. "Every so often, when I hug or kiss her, she makes a little joke about how I do not need to love her so much. It's funny and we both laugh."

We've heard many stories from women like Cindy about moving beyond self-criticism and accepting how they've mothered their daughters. One respondent told us that she recently came to understand how much she had been living through her daughter's accomplishments. "It used to matter to me that my daughter was successful in whatever she did. Even when she was little, I loved bragging about her, and as she grew older, I kept doing it. But I didn't notice how restless and unhappy she was becoming in her work and her marriage, because I was basking in the reflected light of her life. So when she announced she was leaving both her marriage and her job, I was shocked."

Precipitated by this crisis, the mother came to realize that she hadn't been the supportive, listening presence her daughter had needed during her life and especially during this recent tumultuous period. "In truth I was thinking more about myself than her. I was so focused on her success that I ignored the signs of her unhappiness. At the time I thought I was being helpful by encouraging her to overlook what was wrong, but I didn't realize how my comments were putting her under pressure."

We ask her to describe how she came to understand this dynamic. "My daughter was visiting me after her breakup, and tears came to her eyes when I asked her how she was doing. I quickly said something like I was sure she'd get back on track because she's always been so successful. I meant to be reassuring but she just looked at me in a 'you've-got-to-be-kidding' way, and I knew at once how inappropriate my response had been. I immediately apologized and began to think more critically about how I had always laid the burden of success on her. I chastised myself as the most insensitive mother in the world and felt miserable for a long while afterwards. But in the interim, my daughter began to knit her life back together, and as I watched her do this, I knew I also had given her some of the strength that was sustaining her. I hadn't completely failed her."

"Have you ever spoken to her about this?" we ask.

"I'd like to, but it intimidates me," she replies. "Maybe one day."

Apologies

It takes a great deal of courage for mothers to begin a conversation with their daughters about how they failed them. Especially if there isn't a crisis taking center stage and the relationship is moving along in its usual way.

One woman we interviewed confirmed the difficulty of doing this. "I always have been a strong, prideful, stubborn person, and I can see now all the ways this has affected both my daughters. I look back at my younger self and feel ashamed. I was like an immovable force, and when I try to figure out why, I have a few ideas, but none of them balances out or excuses the fact that my daughters had to suffer from my inflexibility."

She continues, "I know I need to talk to my daughters and own up to the ways I wasn't a better mother. They deserve that from me. I'm just struggling to find the right words and the right time. I want the conversation to go well. It's been decades in coming."

Some women decide to put off apologizing to their daughters because they feel they or their daughters are not ready. Margo, with all her feelings of guilt, has considered speaking to Elise about her many regrets, but she holds back. "When I was meditating recently, I had the fantasy of acknowledging every bad thing I had done to her as her mother. I imagined her taking me into her arms and absolving me of all my guilt.

It was a beautiful image—but I knew it wasn't real, or possible, or even desirable. I wasn't ready yet to say those words because I wanted too much from her in return. I'd be doing it to relieve my own guilt, and that's not okay."

"Would she be ready to hear an apology from you?"

Margo hesitates before answering. "Maybe it would help her—or maybe it would just disturb her. I don't know."

We spoke to a mother with a perplexing, on-again, off-again relationship with her daughter. "On a recent visit to her home in Denver, I noticed that I was only in two of the dozens of family photographs she has hung on the walls. At first I felt hurt, but then I realized I have been absent from her and her family's lives, so the lack of my presence in the photos shouldn't be surprising. My daughter's in-laws live close by, and they're the ones who have gone to all the music recitals and school graduations and helped her out when she needed it." The mother sighs. "How sad that I have always been too busy or involved in my own affairs to take the time to travel to Denver more than once or twice a year to be with my own daughter. I can't make up for the past, but I decided I could at the very least tell her how sorry I was about it. I wrote her a long letter, not an email."

"How did you feel after you mailed it?" we ask.

"Very relieved. She's never said anything about getting the letter, but that's okay. The point was for me to write those things down and share my feelings. Since then things have seemed a little easier between us. Or at least I feel more resolved and connected to her. I've called her a little more frequently to check in, and she seems to like that."

Another mother told us how cathartic it had been to apologize to her daughter. "We were walking on a beach in

Malibu and I blurted out that I was sorry I had not been there more for her when she was growing up. It was windy and I kept on talking, saying I realized I'd been unaware of her needs and how that must have been hard for her. Her first response was to be suspicious. 'What am I supposed to do? Tell you it didn't matter?' But I kept on apologizing, saying I wasn't looking for reassurance, and she finally began to listen. I told her I'd abdicated some of my responsibilities as a mother, putting her in the position of taking care of her younger siblings. I'd relied on her too much and was too involved in my own dreams to keep track of ordinary daily tasks like giving her and her sibs lunch money. As I expressed my regret about this, I could see that she was moved by what I was saying. Tears were running down both our cheeks by that time, and we stopped and hugged. It was one of the closest moments we've had."

Forgiving Ourselves and Our Daughters

Some women reach a point where they are able to forgive themselves. Having accepted and acknowledged the difficulties they've caused for their daughters and more clearly understanding their part in their troubled relationships, they are beginning to feel at peace within themselves. Many have taken the brave step of apologizing to their daughters.

"Yes, I made mistakes. A lot of them," Gloria says. "And I'm still making them, though I try to be careful. Even with Kris, my easiest child, I can get off track and become too directive, but she and I have talked about how hard that is for her, and she is able to stop me. For instance, just last night we were on the phone and she was describing the frustration she feels with her boss who is micromanaging and critical. I started making suggestions, having worked myself under so many similar bosses at Child Protection Services, but I got carried away with the elaborations of what she might do. She finally broke into my monologue, saying she just wanted me to listen to her and not solve her problem. I said, 'Oops,' and we both laughed."

Gloria smiles. "Afterwards I felt good about this interaction. She knows and loves me for who I am, a bossy mother sometimes, and we both understand that I'm not always tuned in to what she needs. When I was younger, I would have criticized myself for not listening to her vent last night, but now I don't take those kinds of things so seriously."

"What about with Leanne?" we ask.

"I have a long way to go there," Gloria says. "When I do something that annoys her, I beat up on myself because I fear I've made things worse. She doesn't forgive my mistakes and neither do I."

When mothers are more forgiving of themselves, they feel less weighed down by the past. One mother told us that she used to obsess about the distance between herself and her daughter and blamed herself for causing it. But in recent years she has recognized the ways in which her daughter also has contributed to this painful lack of connection. "It's a great sorrow for me that we're not closer, and I probably will never fully understand why, but acknowledging both sides of this standoff allows me to release the haunted and self-blaming feelings I've carried."

The turning point was when a friend confronted her about how she was allowing her unhappiness about her daughter to take over her life. "I realized I needed to have a more forgiving attitude toward myself. My relationship with my daughter was strained, but that didn't mean I had to be so miserable. I began to stop blaming myself and remember all the good things in the rest of my life. Gradually I had more energy to volunteer at the homeless center and take a Spanish class. It's a process: two steps forward, one backward. But if and when my daughter is ready to see me more often, she'll find a livelier, happier mother welcoming her back."

Forgiveness, mothers say, goes two ways—forgiving themselves and forgiving their daughters. For some mothers, the latter is the hardest because they've been badly wounded by their daughters and find it very difficult to let go of past hurt and anger.

Dolores is such a mother, and toward the end of our long conversation, she speaks of forgiveness. "I don't think I've completely forgiven Yolanda for who she is and her lack of respect and attachment to me," she says. "But every so often I remember her as the forlorn little girl who huddled in her grandmother's arms for comfort as I walked out the door to go to work. And she also must have been disappointed that living together in Oakland didn't work out. I've not been a trustworthy, stable mother, and even though she's used to my absence and seems not to want to have anything to do with me, the lack of a mother's care still must sting. Especially since we come from such a large woven-together family." Dolores pauses. "When I think of all that history, I feel more forgiving. But then, when she doesn't want to have anything to do with me, my good intentions dissolve, and I'm back to being angry at her for being so rejecting."

A big part of forgiving daughters is accepting them fully as they are. One mother we interviewed describes how this works for her. "My daughter could be a beautiful woman, but she doesn't take care of herself. Her nails and hair are unkempt, she dresses in baggy clothing, and she slouches when she walks. Those things have bothered me terribly through the years because I know she could present herself better, but I've come to accept that her way is different from mine. When I let go of thinking that she should be like me and care how she looks, I'm able to be more forgiving and accepting of her. She's a kind and loving woman. It's a matter of seeing beneath to what is truly there. Now, when we're together, I've focused on who she is, not her appearance."

Another woman tells us that she gets along better with her daughter now that she has let go of expectations that will never be met. Her daughter spends long hours working, even on the weekends, and doesn't give her husband and kids much attention. Meals, chores, homework, and housework are always up for grabs. The mother was judgmental about this but also knew that her daughter is a hard worker and happiest out in the world at her job. Once she realized her family wasn't complaining and the household was functioning as well as any other, the mother finally let go of the pressure inside herself to do or say something that would get her daughter to change. Now she feels more relaxed with her, more accepting.

Forgiveness of daughters can take a long time, as Florence understands. "It's not something that happens all at once," she says. "There are still things I find hard to forgive about Rhonda. She's an angry, frustrated woman, and even though I feel sympathy for her, she's sometimes very hard to be around. I've had to let go of my irritation time and time again. Last

Easter at our family dinner, she got mad and exploded at me with so much pent-up emotion I almost fell over. I nearly responded in kind, but something stopped me. I took a breath and decided to listen, just listen, and told everyone at the table to be quiet and let her speak. She went on for a while before petering out and beginning to cry. Everyone at the table remained silent as I told her how sorry I was that she suffers so much and hugged her for a long time. I couldn't have done that if I wasn't also forgiving her."

Changed by Daughters

While sifting through and reviewing their lives, women often become more aware and appreciative of what they have learned from those they love. Their greatest teachers, some say, have been their daughters. The lessons they received were hard or even painful to absorb but helped to shape who they became.

At the end of our interviews, we asked each woman how mothering their daughters has changed who they have become. For some the answers come easily, while others take a while to consider. Their responses are different, but most are accompanied with a sense of gratitude for what they've received from their daughters.

"Terri has made me tougher," Pat says. "She doesn't necessarily give me the approval I want, no matter what I do, and I just have to accept that. I've had to look more carefully at myself because of this. I've come to realize I have a habit of trying to get people to like me or think well of me by doing nice things for them. This has been a lifelong pattern."

When we ask Pat to describe what this is like, she talks about a recent visit to her church. "The board president wanted me to chair the committee to deliver food to our sick and needy members, and I had the good sense to decline. In the past I would have agreed to it so that the president would think well of me, even though I didn't want the responsibility and it would have been too much for me with everything else I'm doing. Afterwards I would have kicked myself."

"This happened because of Terri?"

Pat considers our question. "Our relationship opened my eyes to it. Terri, as you know, is the person I love the most in the world, the person who is the closest to me. If I feel at all insecure about her, as I sometimes do, I can get into trying to help her, or bring her things, or give her compliments. But she'll have none of that. She senses my neediness miles away, and it turns her off. It took me a long time to understand why she withdraws at those times, but once I did, I realized her love for me doesn't depend on me figuring out how to please her but on the connection that exists between us. When I absorbed that, I began to relax and be more myself with her."

"And now?"

"It's hard to break that habit, but as I get older, I am doing it less. Sometimes I backslide, like I did by dropping by Terri's house and bringing her that potted plant. When my little offering didn't please her, I felt hurt and even a little angry. I know that wasn't fair to her, and it wasn't good for me. There were too many strings attached to my gift, and I realized that afterwards. I keep learning this lesson over and over again, not only from her but from other people."

Many women say that mothering has helped them be more

accepting. "I wish it were different with Yolanda," Dolores says. "But it isn't, and I've had to learn to accept that." She pauses. "I used to think I was a terrible person because of the mistakes I made as a mother, but now I understand that my intentions were for the most part good. When Yolanda came to live with me in Oakland, I behaved harshly, but just because I was trying to protect her. I couldn't accept that she wanted to be with her grandmother and the rest of the family in San Antonio, not with me. Our relationship hasn't worked well for either of us, and that's a loss for me. But it's not my fault and it's not hers."

"Does understanding this change how you live?" we ask.

"Vince and his daughter are my family now," she says. "They're the ones I love and care for the most, and they're the ones who help me out or I help them. I used to feel guilty about that but don't anymore. Or at least not very much. Yolanda never makes claims on me to be more involved with her than I already am, and when I accept that this is the way it is, I feel freer."

As Dolores speaks, her face relaxes. "I can thank Yolanda for being honest with me and giving me this freedom."

Gloria has a different story to tell about being changed by her mothering. She's learned the importance of keeping her heart open. "I was cynical about families when I first married, given my mother's early death and my father's abuse. I had been hurt so much and had developed a very strong self-protective shell. But having daughters split my heart wide open, and I fell in love with them when they were young. That created a bond that has endured, although it's certainly been challenged."

"Like when Leanne withdrew after the divorce," we note.

"That really broke me up. But I thought then, and I continue to think now, that no matter what happens, I want her to know that I love and care about her. The same for Kris. It's too easy to become rejecting and close off your heart when you're angry—I know because I've done that—but it doesn't do any good. For them or for me."

We look around Gloria's comfortable living room, at the cat stretched over the couch, the photos of friends and family on the mantel, a half-finished jigsaw puzzle on a big table. "How did your daughters teach you this?" we ask.

"Through the wear and tear of our struggles over the years. I can't tell you how many times I've thought of giving up on Leanne. And even, I admit, a few times on Kris. My heart closes down, and I return to the distrust I felt when I was younger and want to run away. But that doesn't feel good, and either Judy nudges me, or I catch what is happening and remind myself to keep my heart open, even when I'm irritated or hurt."

"Is it getting easier for you as time passes?"

"A little, maybe. With age comes wisdom, right? But truthfully, I have to fight against my impulse to close down each time."

Gloria has learned the importance of loving her daughters during hard times, but Margo's situation is very different. "Elise has been the biggest challenge of my life. No doubt about that. I never expected it to be as hard as it is with her," she says.

"What do you think you've learned?" we ask.

Margo fiddles with her wedding ring. "Today I had a session in my office with a couple whose teenaged son is showing signs of depression. They found a suicidal note in his room, and they're naturally concerned and anxious. They asked me what they should do, looking to me to be the expert. Their questions were reasonable, and I could have given them the standard advice or gotten them to talk about the relationships in their family, but instead, I felt like saying, 'How the hell should I know?'"

"What did you say?"

"I expressed sympathy and told them how very hard this must be for them. They both became teary, and I sat quietly with them for a few minutes before we went on. That was probably helpful, but I felt so humble in their presence. This is what I've learned from mothering Elise."

We consider Margo's forty-year career as a therapist. "Humility must be a good thing to have in your profession."

"It's easy to get too self-important as a therapist," she replies. "Clients look up to you and think you know more than you do, and you're tempted to forget your limitations. Humility keeps that from happening. I'm probably a better, more compassionate therapist as a result of the difficulties with Elise." She stops for a moment. "Our difficulties also led me to my Buddhist practice, and I can thank her for that, too. The downside, though, is that I'm left feeling terribly inadequate. Not so much at work but certainly at home. I don't have any answers about how to help Elise, and all I can do is surrender to the situation and let go of trying to change her. My spiritual practice helps me accept this truth and gives me the strength to keep on going."

Margo's work as a therapist has been deeply affected by mothering Elise, and her life has been very much changed. Cindy's relationship to Frida is of a different nature, but she also has learned important lessons.

"I've always plunged into life," Cindy says. "As an artist, I see myself as experimental and creative. I feel pretty good about how I am, although I'm ashamed about the ways I'm disorganized and wish I had done more to develop my career. Frida, however, doesn't understand my way of life and isn't able to see my strengths."

"How has this changed who you have become?"

"Her attitude toward me has made me look more carefully at myself. In the community of artists, people have a certain pride in their creativity and choices about how to live. They sometimes think they are better than more conventional people like Frida. I used to be that way when I was younger, but since I have a daughter who so clearly is logical and concrete, I've come to see the world in a much broader way. I love Frida, and I can't be a snob toward her or write her off as too uptight or establishment. She's helped me enlarge my world vision."

Cindy points at a small painting on her wall, an intriguing mix of geometric patterns and bright splashes of color. "I did that about ten years ago when I began to understand that Frida and I are very different but both part of a larger reality. She's a geometric person, and I'm a color person—but see how the two go together here? It's not your usual mix, but it works."

We tell Cindy how much we like her painting, and for a moment she looks dreamily out the window at the sun setting over the Pacific Coastal Mountains a few miles to the west. "I'm so moved when I think of Frida and me, two tiny specks of life in this huge universe. We're both part of a great sacred oneness, and the ways we're not alike don't matter at all. It's such a beautiful reality."

We're quiet for a moment, taking in the sunset with Cindy.

"Does your spiritual understanding affect the rest of your life?" we ask.

"It makes everything so much more filled with meaning. And it helps me accept and appreciate differences in everyday life," she replies. "The woman I've fallen in love with is a bit like this painting, a mix of left-brain and right-brain. She's far more together than I am but also very open to the artistic process and an artist herself. One of the reasons we're getting along so well is that I accept and appreciate those parts of her that are more like Frida. If we end up moving to Mexico together, she will be much more capable than me in handling the arrangements."

Cindy feels that her world vision has expanded and she is better able to deal with differences because of being a mother to Frida. When we ask Florence the same question, she answers that she can't lump her two daughters together because they have such different personalities.

"With Rhonda, I have learned to hang in with her," she tells us. "I never expected to have a daughter who was so much work. She sets me on edge with her temper and her moods, and as I said before, I have to remember to listen to her and show her more love," Florence stops for a moment to drink the last sips of her tea. "Patience. That's what I'm still learning with Rhonda. In my lifetime I've been a leader. I was the oldest child in my family, the head of my university department, and on many boards. I'm used to being in charge and having people do as I suggest. But I can't be that way with Rhonda. I have to let her take the lead and be sensitive to her. I have to be patient. I suppose that's a good thing to learn, but it isn't easy."

Florence's cell phone rings, and she excuses herself for a moment. We see her smile as she says hello to Harriet then tells her she'll call back. "That daughter's a different story," she says to us. "She's pure joy, always has been."

We ask her to tell us how being Harriet's mother has changed her. "I don't know that it's made me different since she's always been such an easy child. But she gives me faith and hope that the generations that come after me will do good work. She's committed to the same things I am, her beliefs are strong and they guide her, and I know she'll continue making significant contributions in the future. I'm very proud of her." Florence settles back in her chair. "I can say that Harriet has taught me a lot about love. She greets me warmly when she calls, and she showers me with goodness when she visits. I'm not the easiest person to love because I don't always let it in, but with her, I do. My heart swells, and I'm so grateful she's my daughter."

Moving Forward

Over the course of our conversations with mothers of middle-aged daughters, we have learned a great deal about how they understand their relationships. They care deeply about their daughters, and most yearn to be close and connected to them. Sometimes this desire is fulfilled, but at other times they are disappointed or hurt by more distance than they would like. The issues that emerge are numerous and varied, and mothers struggle to handle them, often faltering, sometimes succeeding. Many feel they need to hide or diminish parts of themselves to get along with their daughters, and as they move into the last decades of their lives, they face issues of future diminishment and dependency. Mothering midlife daughters is a challenge, yet most have powerful, intense feelings about these relationships and consider them to be the most significant, or among the most significant, in their lives.

As we speak with mothers, we are struck by the complexity of these relationships. We learn about their childhoods, seen as being formative to how they have been as mothers, and we hear about their expectations when they gave birth to their daughters in the explosive cultural and political climate of the sixties and seventies. We follow their marriages, divorces, partnerships, work, creative ventures, values, and commitments through the years. They tell us of the early family years with their daughters when they were young, the love, connection, anger, and regret, and we hear about the many issues that arose after they grew up and left home.

All of this is present as mothers search for understanding about their connection to their daughters toward the end of their lives. For many, there is hard work to be done. Confronting events that have been kept in the shadows may elicit waves of guilt or sorrow, and letting go of judgments frozen into painful certainty can be a destabilizing process. But the task for mothers is to look at these relationships as they are today and understand how they developed so they can come to terms with what exists in the here and now.

For some, there is an effort to mend or heal what remains troubled with their daughters. Apologies are offered, or words of truth are finally spoken, or attempts are made to reach out in new and different ways. Other mothers come to the point of accepting their relationships as they are, either because they're satisfied with them or because acceptance seems to be the best or the only course. Sometimes those who are distant or estranged from their daughters find themselves letting go and accepting that there will be no change.

As mothers search for the unique meanings of past, present, and future, the healing that takes place sometimes feels spiritual in nature. They now have a larger, fuller sense of time extending before their lives began and continuing after its end, and they say this softens the reckoning.

One woman described her different sense of time in this way: "I need to wear knee pads in the garden now, but I still spend hours there, kneeling before the growing things I've planted. I weed, prune, and delight in the richness of the life that surrounds me. If I had to define my spirituality, this would be what it looks like: planting and nourishing life, delighting in the variety of shapes and colors that emerge, and knowing that these living things will continue long after I'm gone. I feel the same way about my daughters. Like variegated plants, each has her own weed-filled roots that need periodic clearing, and each blossoms with its unique colors and shapes. They, their children, and all those who come after them will represent what I have put into motion. This comforts me and gives me a sense of my place in the ongoing mystery of life."

Coming to terms with one's mistakes, poor judgments, and misplaced priorities takes a certain kind of fearlessness. Courage is required whether mothers try to heal their relationships or accept them. It is difficult to speak honestly to a beloved daughter and painful to fully accept a disappointing, distant relationship, knowing that this is all there ever will be.

Yet the mothers we speak with have a great deal of strength as they move through this time of reckoning. They report feeling bolder and more confident than they did as younger women, and some have dramatically altered their ways of relating to their daughters. Others have softened old patterns, and most have come to an awareness of the importance of being their best selves with their daughters. They seem to have become smarter about their mothering now and able to shift into the role of loving accompaniment rather than one of leadership.

They have learned that there are few epiphanies, but sometimes change can and does happen. The process of life assessment and reflection is an ongoing one. Mothers do not discover new and improved problem-solving techniques but instead recognize their ability to tolerate different kinds of conversations with their daughters. There are fewer repetitions of the unsuccessful efforts of the past, and they have an expanded capacity to hear and become open to their daughters in less defensive ways.

They realize that they and their daughters reach for each other in ways that sometimes feel disconnected, and this process is endless. When talking about their relationships, the word "healing" is not quite right to express what they are doing—it's more redemption or understanding. That which is broken has been revealed and will be carried forward.

Mothers know now that everything need not be said. The past exists, but it is not excavated with the exactitude they once imagined was necessary. They are less attached to words and more open to the flow of feeling, and they intuit what is being expressed by a silent nod, a hand laid gently upon an arm, a smiling refill of a coffee cup. Words are sometimes a necessary bridge, but they are more carefully considered.

The relationships of mothers with their daughters will never be finished or resolved completely. But in the meanwhile, they cherish and hold on to them or they mourn their absence. They are flesh of their flesh, the most precious of beings. They are with them all their years, a gift, sometimes breaking their hearts but also bringing satisfaction and fulfillment in this most human of worlds.

DISCUSSION QUESTIONS

1. Mothers define closeness and distance with their daughters in a wide range of ways. How would you describe the form it takes with your daughter? How is it expressed? If you have more than one daughter, how does it differ with each of them?

2. In what ways are you and your daughter similar or different? How does that affect your relationship?

3. The experience women had with their own mothers influenced what kind of mothers they tried to be when their daughters were born in the mid-20th century. How did your childhood define how you mothered? What did you reject or pass on to your daughter? Did becoming a mother change your connection with your own mother?

4. How is your relationship with your daughter affected by your personal history and the choices you made through the years? What do you see as the mistakes you made? What are your strengths as a mother? How has the relationship been affected by the experience of divorce, blended families, your changing roles? How is the past being acted out in the present?

5. What are the ways in which you are still mothering? Are they concrete, like caring for a grandchild or providing financial support, or more fluid, like serving as a sounding board? What do you have to give to your daughter at this time in your life? Is your mothering satisfying?

6. What are the obstacles to having the kind of relationship you want with your middle-aged daughter? What issues arise between you and how are they navigated? How do you deal with anger, resentment, envy, and competitiveness, and where do you and she get stuck?

7. Where are your hesitations about moving too close to a subject that may be sensitive? Who decides what is off-limits? What forms of communication work best with your daughter, and where are your necessary silences?

8. Mothers describe ongoing vigilance about what they share about themselves and their lives with their daughter. Many find it difficult to speak honestly and directly for fear of disrupting their connection. Do you remain silent in order to keep things secure between you and your daughter? About what subjects? What do you wish you could express to her or hear from her?

9. Mothers say these are the years of taking stock, putting their affairs in order, and beginning the preparations for the last stages of life. How are you thinking about your own aging? What decisions have you made about housing, finances, and your end-of-life wishes, and how have they been communicated to your daughter? Are you able to remain open and authentic about all the changes ahead—physical, psychological, and financial?

10. As mothers age, they can experience a growing sense of courage. Historic self-protective stories ascribing blame and responsibility begin to soften, and mothers can become more willing to look squarely at their responsibility for

what may have gone wrong with their daughters and begin to think about how to repair what has been broken or frayed. This is described in the book as a time of reckoning. What defines your own sense of reckoning?

11. The final question we asked all our respondents was, "How has mothering your daughter changed who you have become?" How would you respond?

We want to hear from each of you who has read *It Never Ends: Mothering Middle-Aged Daughters*. Our intention in writing the book was to open a conversation among women who had never before had a place in which they could think aloud and communicate with one another about their experience as aging mothers. We will honor the confidentiality of your communication as we have for all mothers who have allowed us into their lives.

You can share your stories, reflections, and responses to this book by contacting us at:

motheringdaughters@gmail.com

or writing us at:

It Never Ends
1534 Campus Drive
Berkeley, CA 94708

ACKNOWLEDGMENTS

This book was born out of the writing of generations of scholars and activists who focused attention on the daily realities of women's lives. We are grateful to them for their insistence that we speak about our experiences in our own words. We want to thank the seventy-eight women who sat with us and excavated some of the most complex, painful aspects of their lives. We appreciate their courage and candor in describing their relationships with their daughters, the mistakes they made, their love for them, and their desire for healing and closeness. We are also grateful to the dozens of women who informally told us about their experience as mothers once they heard about our project. Their insights deepened our thinking, and their enthusiasm underscored the need for this book.

It was a great pleasure to work with the women at She Writes Press. Thanks especially go to the publisher, Brooke Warner, for guiding this process, to Cait Levin for her meticulous attention to tracking the many details involved in ushering our book into the world, and to the community of She Writes authors, an ingathering of writers and readers par excellence.

We are both members of a longstanding women's group that has provided a central framework for much of our thinking and questioning over the five years it took to complete our manuscript. We thank Jane Ariel, Marinell Eva, Marcia Freedman, and Linda Wilson for sharing their thoughts about mothering with us and their encouragement and support.

We are grateful to our friends and colleagues for their engagement during this time: Adrianne and Mike Bank, Chana Bloch z"l, Lorraine Bonner, Sandy Boucher, Ellen and Patrick Coffey, Jeri Cohen, Donna Korones, Susan and Charlie Halpern, Jan Holmgren, Naomi Newman, Penny Rosenwasser, Nancy Stoller, Mia Tenenberg, and Kaethe Weingarten.

Our great thanks go to the members of our birth and chosen families for giving us the space to write this book and encouraging us with kind words and distractions when we became overwhelmed with the task: Kirk Allen, Nathan Allen, Elias Allen, Nicole Bloom, Evan Blumensweig, Bill Holstein, Sarah Holstein, Jackie Holstein, Tim McAlee, Nick Piediscalzi, Jack Piediscalzi, and Sue Swigart. Special appreciation goes to Jonathan Omer-Man for his ideas, patience, and support.

Most especially we are grateful to our daughters, Alison Butler, Michelle Holstein, Janaea McAlee, and Lisa Piediscalzi. They are our teachers and guides, precious to us beyond words.

photo credit: Irene Young

SANDRA BUTLER is the author of *Conspiracy of Silence: The Trauma of Incest.* Her second book, *Cancer in Two Voices,* coauthored with Barbara Rosenblum, was the winner of the 1991 Lambda Literary Award. She is also the co-producer of the award-winning documentaries *Cancer in Two Voices* and *Ruthie and Connie: Every Room in the House.* She has two middle-aged daughters and a rich community of women friends.

NAN FINK GEFEN is the author of *Stranger in the Midst: A Memoir of Spiritual Discovery, Discovering Jewish Meditation,* and *Clear Lake: A Novel,* winner of the IndieFab Gold Award for general fiction. After fifteen years in practice as a psychotherapist, she became the co-founding publisher in 1986 of *Tikkun* magazine, a journal of politics, culture, and society. In 2007 she founded *Persimmon Tree: An Online Magazine of the Arts by Women Over Sixty,* where she remains as publisher. Nan lives with her husband in Berkeley CA. Their blended family includes seven children and ten grandchildren.

SELECTED TITLES FROM SHE WRITES PRESS

She Writes Press is an independent publishing company founded to serve women writers everywhere. Visit us at www.shewritespress.com.

Stepmother: A Memoir by Marianne Lile. $16.95, 978-1-63152-089-1. Lile describes the complexities of the stepmom position, in a family and in the community, and shares her experience wearing a tag that is often misunderstood and weighed down by the numerous myths in society.

Warrior Mother: A Memoir of Fierce Love, Unbearable Loss, and Rituals that Heal by Sheila K. Collins, PhD. $16.95, 978-1-938314-46-9. The story of the lengths one mother goes to when two of her three adult children are diagnosed with potentially terminal diseases.

Filling Her Shoes: Memoir of an Inherited Family by Betsy Graziani Fasbinder. $16.95, 978-1-63152-198-0. A "sweet-bitter" story of how, with tenderness as their guide, a family formed in the wake of loss and learned that joy and grief can be entwined cohabitants in our lives.

Splitting the Difference: A Heart-Shaped Memoir by Tré Miller-Rodríguez. $19.95, 978-1-938314-20-9. When 34-year-old Tré Miller-Rodríguez's husband dies suddenly from a heart attack, her grief sends her on an unexpected journey that culminates in a reunion with the biological daughter she gave up at 18.

Don't Leave Yet: How My Mother's Alzheimer's Opened My Heart by Constance Hanstedt. $16.95, 978-1-63152-952-8. The chronicle of Hanstedt's journey toward independence, self-assurance, and connectedness as she cares for her mother, who is rapidly losing her own identity to the early stage of Alzheimer's.

The Space Between: A Memoir of Mother-Daughter Love at the End of Life by Virginia A. Simpson. $16.95, 978-1-63152-049-5. When a life-threatening illness makes it necessary for Virginia Simpson's mother, Ruth, to come live with her, Simpson struggles to heal their relationship before Ruth dies.